THE BOOK OF
BASTARDS

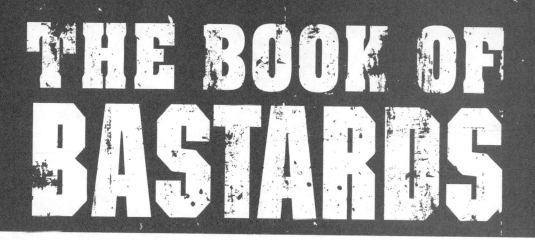

THE BOOK OF BASTARDS

★★★★ 101 **WORST**
Scoundrels
and Scandals
FROM THE WORLD OF
POLITICS
AND POWER

★ **BRIAN THORNTON** ★

Aadamsmedia
Avon, Massachusetts

Published by
Adams Media, a division of F+W Media, Inc.
57 Littlefield Street, Avon, MA 02322. U.S.A.
www.adamsmedia.com

ISBN 10: 1-4405-0370-2
ISBN 13: 978-1-4405-0370-2
eISBN 10: 1-4405-0738-4
eISBN 13: 978-1-4405-0738-0

Printed in the United States of America.

10 9 8 7 6 5 4 3 2 1

Library of Congress Cataloging-in-Publication Data
Thornton, Brian
Book of bastards / Brian Thornton.
p. cm.
Includes bibliographical references and index.
ISBN-13: 978-1-4405-0370-2 (alk. paper)
ISBN-10: 1-4405-0370-2 (alk. paper)
ISBN-13: 978-1-4405-0738-0 (e)
ISBN-10: 1-4405-0738-4 (e)
1. United States—Biography—Miscellanea. 2. Politicians—United States—Biography—Miscellanea. 3.
Presidents—United States—Biography—Miscellanea. 4. Legislators—United States—Biography—Miscellanea. 5.
United States—Politics and government—Miscellanea. 6. United States—History—Miscellanea. I. Title.
E176.T575 2010
973.09'9—dc22
2010009948

This publication is designed to provide accurate and authoritative information with regard to the subject matter covered. It is sold with the understanding that the publisher is not engaged in rendering legal, accounting, or other professional advice. If legal advice or other expert assistance is required, the services of a competent professional person should be sought.
—From a *Declaration of Principles* jointly adopted by a Committee of the American Bar Association and a Committee of Publishers and Associations

Many of the designations used by manufacturers and sellers to distinguish their product are claimed as trademarks. Where those designations appear in this book and Adams Media was aware of a trademark claim, the designations have been printed with initial capital letters.

This book is available at quantity discounts for bulk purchases.
For information, please call 1-800-289-0963.

ACKNOWLEDGMENTS

A book is a collaborative work, no matter how many names appear on the cover. This book is no different, and I have a lot of people to thank.

First, to Robyn: thank you for your help with the vetting of our cast of singular villains, for your feedback on so many of these entries, and especially for your spirited defense of Thomas Jefferson right to the very end. Most importantly, thank you for marrying me. This book is dedicated to you.

Thanks also to Joe Hylkema: your research and suggestions (especially surrounding the Enron mess) in support of the later pages of this book was invaluable. You make a much better skeptic than you ever did a "true believer," pal.

To my parents, Hal and Berniece, and my brother, Paul: thanks for putting up with this project and the way it consumed whole conversations at so many family gatherings. I am truly blessed to have family like you.

To my editor and my friend, Paula Munier at Adams Media, who gave me my first book contract six years ago, and whose enthusiasm for this book has never flagged since I first pitched the idea to her. Thanks Paula, and to all the people at Adams Media. You're a great bunch.

CONTENTS

INTRODUCTION

The German poet Rainer Maria Rilke once wrote: "If my devils are to leave me, I am afraid my angels will take flight as well." It is a testament to the duality of human nature that notions such as "good" and "evil" have little meaning without their opposite number to lend them context.

It is also true that human beings tend to be mixed bags. Evil people can acknowledge truth and beauty, and of course be moved to acts of kindness: the Roman emperor Nero loved the arts, Adolf Hitler adored children and dogs, and so on. The opposite is also the case. You'll find among the thoroughgoing bastards who populate the pages of this book some truly "Great Men" in the classical meaning of the phrase.

And while it's true that J. Pierpont Morgan was a silver-spoon-sucking son-of-a-bitch who cheated his own government by selling them defective rifles *during wartime*, he also helped found the Metropolitan Museum of Art so that people who could never dream of purchasing one of the statues that populate that institution's Greek and Roman wing could enjoy these testaments to human creativity as he did.

In many cases the tales of bastardry contained herein will titillate, perhaps even scandalize the reader. In others, where the "bastard" in question has an otherwise positive image, the revelation of that person's "bastard" side will hopefully offer some context to the character of the "bastard" in question.

After all, everyone loves hearing about an out-and-out bastard. That's likely because everyone has a little bit of the bastard in them: and some of our greatest leaders have allowed their "inner bastard" to inform their decisions for both good and ill. In this book you'll find some outright bastards with no redeeming qualities. You'll also find some otherwise good people who let their "inner bastard" get the better of them.

Devils or angels, in the end it's all about the choices.

★1★
LORD DE LA WARR:
How to Steal Land from the Indians and Keep It "Legal"
(1577–1618)

"A more damned crew hell never vomited."
—George Sandys, Virginia Company treasurer, on the quality of the settlers at Jamestown in 1623

One of history's most time-honored ways to acquire property is to simply take it from others. Depending on who tells the story, this is usually described as either "conquest" or as "theft." No country lacks a land grab story, and the United States is no exception. With this longstanding tradition in mind, it only makes sense to start off a book documenting corrupt practices in America with the burn-and-kill tactics of Jamestown governor Lord De La Warr.

In a matter of three short years, England's Jamestown colony lost all but sixty of its original settlers to disease, starvation, and more frequent Indian attacks. Only the timely arrival of newly appointed governor Thomas West, Lord De La Warr, kept the original colonists from leaving the site. Our first bastard landed with provisions and backup, ready to save the New World.

BASTARD BACKGROUND

In the centuries before Columbus, Native Americans fought for the best land, pretty much like anyone else. The Celts, Romans, Aryans, and Persians are just a few Old World counterparts known for taking what wasn't rightfully theirs. By the time Europeans began to explore the Americas, stealing land was a normal part of human history. The first English settlers, however, weren't your typical honest, hard-working colonists. Most of the five hundred men who came to the New World were so-called "gentlemen," second sons (if that) of landed aristocrats. In reality this bunch of lazy, mean-spirited bastards were only interested in finding hoards of Indian gold as the Spanish had in Mexico and Peru. These first English settlers were brutal, ignorant, and land-hungry, scornful of the "inferior" Indians; the Indians for their part returned the compliments. You can guess what happened next.

Lord De La Warr proved to be Jamestown's salvation, but the surrounding Native American tribes bore most of the heavy costs involved. De La Warr learned how to take land when he fought in England's ongoing battles with the Irish. His methods were similar to the ones Indians used in their wars with the English and each other, but history gave De La Warr's version a special name. He freely employed these so-called "Irish tactics" against the Powhatans and the other local Algonquian tribes. Under De La Warr's command, the colonists raided Indian towns, stealing crops, burning cornfields. They set a scene that replayed itself along the American frontier over the next three centuries.

We can find plenty to dislike about the prime movers on both sides of this long struggle between early American bastards. It is worth noting, though, that the man who started the trend was De La Warr, the English lord and military man. In one of history's ironies, De La Warr failed to profit from his ruthlessness in securing the future of the Virginia Colony. His mission of saving Jamestown from extinction accomplished, De La Warr set sail for England in 1618. He died during the return voyage, and no one is quite sure what became of his body.

"And here in Florida, Virginia, New-England, and Cannada, is more land than all the people in Christendome can manure, and yet more to spare than all the natives of those Countries can use and cultivate. The natives are only too happy to share: If this be not a reason sufficient to such tender consciences; for a copper kettle and a few toyes, as beads and hatchets, they will sell you a whole Country."
—Captain John Smith

★2★
THE PURITANS
Not Just More Pilgrims

> "But for the natives in these parts, God hath so pursued them, as for 300 miles space the greatest part of them are swept away by smallpox which still continues among them. So as God hath thereby cleared our title to this place, those who remain in these parts, being in all not 50, have put themselves under our protection."
> —John Winthrop

Don't confuse the Pilgrims and Puritans: these English religious sects were more different than their names would lead you to believe. The first group arrived in North America and treated the local Indians civilly. The others treated the native people as an obstacle to be removed, conquered, or converted.

The Pilgrims, outsiders that they were, left England for Holland, but soon after decided that their children would be less likely to lose their "Englishness" in a new land than in the Low Countries. A large group of them departed for the New World in 1620. They founded Plymouth Plantation that same year. The Puritans followed them soon afterward, founding Boston in 1630, and quickly outnumbering their separatist neighbors.

In no time at all the Puritans ran into trouble with the native peoples. They were determined to convert the locals into Christian, "Praying Indians." The neighboring Pequot, Narragansett, and Wampanoag tribes were naturally reluctant to change their ways of life for the strangers. The Puritans, of course, met resistance with violence. In 1637, just seven years after the founding of Boston, the Puritans went to war with the most numerous tribe in the region at the time, the Pequots. Within the year, more than 1,500 Indians were dead and the Pequots had all but ceased to exist as an independent tribal entity.

The Puritans repeated this cycle with the Wampanoag in the 1660s and 1670s. The Pilgrims and the Wampanoag sachem (chief) Massasoit had gotten along very well. But Massasoit's son Metacomet, known as "King Philip" by the Puritans, fought the Puritans in King Philip's War from 1675–6.

Both sides in the war favored fire as a weapon. Indians retreating into their great walled towns quickly learned that the Puritans had no compunctions about burning their homes down around their ears. One group of Praying Indians was murdered when their church was burned down with them still inside. The culprits? Not other Indians taking revenge on religious traitors, but Puritan settlers, their own coreligionists! It is not surprising that many Indian attacks on Puritan settlements resulted in similar treatment.

THE BACKGROUND

The Pilgrims and the Puritans were both groups of English Christians who were dissenters from the mainstream Church of England. The Pilgrims were separatists, in other words, people who sought freedom to worship apart from the Church of England and to establish their own church. Today, they are known as the Congregationalists. The Puritans, on the other hand, didn't want to leave the church. They wanted to "purify" it from within: hence their nickname. The Puritans believed they needed to purge anything related to Catholicism from their Protestant faith and lifestyle in order to avoid eternal damnation.

By the time it had run its course this war resulted in nearly four thousand deaths (three thousand of them Indians, including King Philip), an incredibly high toll considering the number of colonists at the time. The Wampanoag and their allies were wiped out. Those Indians not killed by disease, bullets, or torches were sold into slavery in places such as the West Indies and Bermuda. And this included most of the Praying Indians. The native population crippled, the Puritans claimed lands now open to settlement as God-sent blessings for their piety.

Pious Bastards.

★3★

THOMAS PENN
The Pennsylvania Walking Purchase, or How to Steal Land from the Indians and Keep It "Legal": The Sequel
(1702–1775)

> "William Penn was a wise and good man, but Thomas was a miserable churl."
> —Benjamin Franklin

William Penn, the founder of the colony of Pennsylvania (Latin for "Penn's Woods"), was a nonconformist. A man both of peace and of his word, Penn dealt straightforwardly with the local Indians. He treated them as he would have any other human being and paid them for lands they relinquished to the settlers of his new colony. The Lenape, the largest and most powerful of these tribes, enjoyed particularly good relations with Penn. They referred to him as their father and honored him as they would their own chiefs.

William Penn died in 1718, struggling to make ends meet after spending a great deal of money on his colony. He was succeeded as "proprietor" of Pennsylvania by his second son, Thomas. Thomas Penn turned out to be a very different man from his father. He was proof that, in the case of the Penn family, the old adage "the apple doesn't fall too far from the tree" hardly applied. Where the elder Penn had been determined to build something admirable and not all that concerned with profit, his son was determined to profit and not all that concerned with being admirable. No other example spells out the difference between William Penn and his son than that of the infamous Walking Purchase of 1737.

Most of the Pennsylvania colony's settlements were restricted to the Delaware River Valley's west bank, stretching no more than a few miles inland. Penn's agents produced an unsigned and likely forged treaty supposedly dating back to 1688 that would change Pennsylvania for good. According to the "treaty," Lenape chiefs had agreed to sell the Penns a parcel of their lands from the junction of the Lehigh and Delaware Rivers and continuing "as far west as a man could walk in a day and a half."

WHY THE BASTARD DID IT

Left land-rich but cash-poor by his father, Thomas Penn married the daughter of an earl, and styled himself as an aristocrat. That sort of "lifestyle" didn't come cheap. The sale of the land stolen in "Ye Hurry Walk" helped make Penn a millionaire, and financed the sort of "lifestyle" to which he thought himself entitled.

The Lenape chiefs weren't happy about the treaty, but felt they had no choice but to agree to what they called "Ye Hurry Walk." They assumed they would sell as much as could be traced by following the Lehigh River along its course westward. Penn, however, had already calculated his claim and sold off parcels of the land he expected to receive in the deal. He hired three professional runners and had his agents clear a road for them to run on. Rather than following the Lehigh River trail, the road would lead the runners due west, deep into Lenape territory. Penn took great care to turn "as far west as a man could walk in a day and a half" into "as far west as I can reach." What followed was the single largest land swindle in colonial American history.

On September 19, 1737, the three runners set off from present-day Wrightstown, Pennsylvania. Only one of the three runners managed to run for the entire allotted time, but he finished seventy miles inland. In one thirty-six-hour period, Thomas Penn stole from the Lenape a land tract the size of the state of Rhode Island (about 3,000 square miles).

As if that weren't enough, Penn later tried to suspend Pennsylvania's colonial assembly and rule by decree. Luckily for the colonists, Benjamin Franklin, already a celebrated American leader, foiled him. Penn retaliated by hiring Franklin's "illegitimate" son as Pennsylvania's governor: a case of a metaphorical bastard hiring an actual one.

★4★
NATHANIEL BACON
His Rebellion
(CA. 1640–1676)

"Here! Shoot me, foregod, fair mark shoot!"
—William Berkeley, Virginia governor, as he confronted Nathaniel Bacon and his band of five hundred rebels, June 22, 1676

Think about it. A group of settlers—nothing more than freehold farmers, really—stood up for their individual rights and shook their collective fists at the landed interests of the British crown and the rich Loyalists. They showed the "Spirit of '76" and took up arms in order to see to it that their families were looked after.

Sounds like the American Revolution, right?

Wrong. The conflict described above played out not in 1776, but a century earlier, in *1676.*

We're talking about Bacon's Rebellion. Bearing the name of the man who provided the lit match to the tinder pile of class resentment and land disputes in late seventeenth-century Virginia, the upheaval both lived and died with its leader and namesake: Nathaniel Bacon. Bacon was a charismatic leader, a brave man under fire, clever politician, and, of course, an absolute bastard.

Bacon's true bastardry began when he moved to Virginia. He used his father's money to purchase two estates right on the James River. With land came instant respectability. A few months later, Bacon had been fully accepted into Virginia society. Lord Berkeley, the husband of Bacon's cousin, had given him a seat on the Governor's Council. But it couldn't last.

By 1674 the cousins-in-law had alienated each other over the question of the direction of the colony's growth. Berkeley favored keeping the frontier where it currently was and not acquiring any more of the lands from the neighboring Indians.

Bacon agreed with the frontier farmers. Together they advocated expanding Virginia's borders westward by driving tribes such as the Pamunkey and Susquehannock off of their native lands. Berkeley just wouldn't relent. So in 1676 Bacon assembled a group of four hundred followers willing to make war on the neighboring tribes. He insisted Berkeley give him an official directive to kill or drive off as many of the Indian residents as possible. When Berkeley refused, Bacon accused Berkeley of corruption. Bacon turned his troops on Jamestown in a full revolt.

BASTARD BACKGROUND

By birth Nathaniel Bacon was the most unlikely of rebels. His family were wealthy members of the local gentry in Suffolk, England, thus Bacon was born a gentleman. By 1672 he developed a reputation as a hothead and a troublemaker. After Bacon was caught trying to cheat a neighbor of his inheritance, his father stepped in and offered Bacon a way out. He would back his son's business venture in one of the New World colonies. The catch: Bacon would have to leave England and go to America if he wished to receive his father's backing. He did so, immigrating to Virginia in 1672.

Berkeley got wind of Bacon's impending attack just in time to flee across Chesapeake Bay to the Eastern Shore county of Accomack. Bacon responded by ordering his followers to burn the governor's palace to the ground, then headed west to make war on the Pamunkeys, Appomatucks, and Susquehannocks. Much blood was shed on both sides.

It was at about this time that Bacon's luck ran out. Stricken down with dysentery (referred to at the time by the charming appellation of the "Bloody Flux"), he died in October, 1676, less than a month after torching the governor's residence.

Without Bacon to lead his rebellion it collapsed. Berkeley returned from Accomack County and quickly restored order. Before the year was out, he had hanged twenty-three of the rebels: the last of the many lives lost on account of that bastard Nathaniel Bacon.

★5★
JAMES DELANCEY
Graft in New York: The Early Years
(1703–1760)

"A Chief Justice known to be of an implacable temper is a terrible
thing in this country."
—Cadwallader Colden about James DeLancey

William Marcy Tweed, Huey Long, William Lorimer, Richard Daley, Tom Pendergast: all famous (or if you prefer, "infamous") political leaders known in America as "bosses." All of them were successful to varying degrees. And yet none of
them could touch the successes enjoyed by America's first political boss. Colonial
New York Governor James DeLancey just had a flair for bastardry unlike any
other.

DeLancey wrote the book on building a political machine and trading influence in American politics. He was a political animal from his birth in 1703.
His father was a prosperous French Huguenot, and his mother was the daughter
of New York City's first native-born mayor Stephen Van Cortlandt. Educated
in England, handsome, intelligent, and witty, DeLancey had a wide network of
familial alliances and set about making even more of them, His tutor at Cam-
bridge eventually became Archbishop of Canterbury. He married an heiress with
connections to prominent London politicians. His sister married British Admiral
Sir Peter Warren. Warren was the hero of the Siege of Louisbourg, a battle where
British forces took the strongest French fort in the Western Hemisphere. This
coup carried Warren into politics. Once established, he used his influence to help
along his brother-in-law's political career.

With the help of his family and friends, DeLancey accomplished a great deal as a young man. He was appointed to New York's Governor's Council at twenty-six. At twenty-eight he'd won a seat on the New York Supreme Court. By thirty he was chief justice. Over the years DeLancey packed the Governor's Council with his own allies. He distributed political favors through his network, building the foundation of a formidable political machine.

WHAT'S THAT WORD? "BOSS"

In his book *A Study in Boss Politics: William Lorimer of Chicago*, author Joel Arthur Tarr defined the phrase "political boss" as "a dictator who represented special and corrupt interests and who violated the rights of 'the people'." Bosses controlled political machines, organizations that did their bidding and shared in the profits (both legal and illegal) that their activities produced.

Efficient and tireless, DeLancey got things done. On the other hand, he could also be a bitter political foe. According to fellow Supreme Court Justice Cadwallader Colden, New York now had a chief justice who used "the power of his office to intimidate" those who opposed him. DeLancey's incessant political maneuvering even resulted in New York's royal governor naming him chief justice for life in 1744. His powerbase now secure, DeLancey began laying plans for his next move: securing the governorship of New York. In 1753 he got it. At times he was "royal governor." Other times, he was "acting governor." The title mattered less than the power.

James DeLancey controlled the executive branch of New York's colonial government until his death in June of 1760. Because of his life-appointment as chief justice of a colonial court packed with his cronies, he also controlled the New York judiciary. And because he spent his first ten years in politics building alliances among both New York City's aldermen and the members of the colonial assembly, he also controlled the colonial legislature. After James DeLancey's death, any political boss that followed could only dream of hitting such a trifecta. Others would work from DeLancey's playbook, but none would ever succeed as he had. DeLancey died of natural causes, still clutching the strings of power, still holding office, still wealthy, and never having served a day in jail.

★6★
GEORGE WASHINGTON
Tenth Commandment? What Tenth Commandment?
(1732–1799)

"'Tis true, I profess myself a Votary to Love—I acknowledge that a Lady is in the Case—and further I confess that this Lady is known to you.—Yes Madam, as well as she is to one, who is too sensible of her Charms to deny the Power, whose Influence he feels and must ever submit to."
—George Washington

Shakespeare? Nope. Wordsworth? Nah. Who is the author of this intensely romantic passage? None other than our most famous president: George Washington. And he didn't write it to his wife, or to just any one of his previous sweethearts. He wrote it as part of an intriguing letter to his best friend's wife.

Before he was president, before he chaired the Constitutional Convention, before he was commander-in-chief of the Continental Army, before he was "George Washington," George Washington was in love with a married woman named Sally Fairfax.

Sally was married to wealthy landowner George William Fairfax. Washington knew the couple through his elder brother Lawrence, who was married to Fairfax's sister.

Washington wrote many letters to Sally, always hinting at something he shouldn't talk about. Later in the same letter quoted above, Washington mentions the futility of his affections, using the same oblique language: "[B]ut experience alas! Sadly reminds me how impossible this is." Still later he hints that there is only one person who can make him happy. He teases that Sally knows this person. He also refers to *Cato*, a contemporary stage play that they had both seen, saying, "I should think my time more agreeable spent believe me, in playing a part in Cato . . . & myself doubly happy in being the Juba to such a Marcia as you must make." This last remark is the most telling. In *Cato*, Juba is a North African prince who is secretly, hopelessly, passionately in love with the title character's daughter, Marcia. Washington obviously had quite a thing for the young, beautiful, popular, and worldly Sally.

⟶ ᔕ ⟵

BASTARD ON THE MAKE

Not only was the "Father of his Country" a horny bastard trying to score with his best friend's wife, he was also perpetually on the lookout to "improve his situation." Speculating in land, romancing girls from wealthy families, and eventually marrying the richest widow in the colony, George Washington was a man on the make before he was the "Man on Horseback."

Did Sally return Washington's affection? We know that they spent much time together, and often outside of the company of her much older husband. The Fairfaxes were the most frequent visitors to Mount Vernon after Washington's marriage. The would-be lovers exchanged letters for the remainder of their lives, even after Washington married and after Sally and her husband moved to England in 1773.

In a much later letter, Washington told Sally how much her company had meant to him. He wrote of how he had "never been able to eradicate from my mind those happy moments, the happiest in my life, which I have enjoyed in your company." The fact of the matter is that whether or not Washington took liberties with Sally, he eventually moved on, married Martha (one of the wealthiest women in Virginia), and by all accounts had a good marriage. Far from being the stolid, "marble statue" that history so often makes of our leaders, Washington was naturally fiery, passionate, and given to great flights of fancy.

So go figure, George Washington, the marble man on horseback, the boring guy on the dollar bill, likely had an affair with his hot young neighbor, and went on to "marry up." Talk about an overachiever! Who knew the guy had so much in common with Bill Clinton?

★7★
BENEDICT ARNOLD
America's First Traitor
(1741–1801)

"Let me die in this old uniform in which I fought my battles. May God forgive me for ever having put on another."
—Benedict Arnold's last words

To this day the name of Benedict Arnold is synonymous with the word "traitor." But who was Benedict Arnold really? Was he as big a bastard as popular history makes him out to be?

Truth be told, Benedict Arnold nearly died in the Battle of Saratoga in 1777. Had he perished on the field that day, he would have come down to us second only to George Washington in esteem. He would likely have been held in wide regard as the greatest battlefield commander on either side of the Revolutionary War.

That said, he was still unquestionably a bastard.

A prosperous Connecticut merchant and experienced sea captain during peacetime, by 1777 Arnold was also a seasoned battlefield commander. Twice-wounded veteran of the seizure of Fort Ticonderoga, the assault on Quebec, the naval battle on Lake Champlain, and a host of other engagements, and George Washington's favorite general.

But even before turning traitor Arnold was a bastard. He possessed a knack for making enemies, and was often accused of corruption and profiteering. He could, at least, foist the blame on his prewar business success operating as a smuggler evading British import duties. But Arnold was also touchy about his honor, had a short fuse, and had fought a number of duels. And as he was never reimbursed for the fortune he spent outfitting troops, Arnold wanted to make back his investment and then some.

By the time Arnold was in command of the American fortifications at West Point in 1780, he was more desperate for new sources of income than ever. He used his young, free-spending wife's loyalist family connections to set up a meeting at which he agreed to turn over West Point to the British. Only the capture of the British officer with whom Arnold had met foiled the plot.

A GLORIOUS BASTARD

In October 1777, the American forces under General Horatio Gates had bottled up the main British force under command of General "Gentleman Johnny" Burgoyne within a day's ride from Albany. On October 7, a pitched battle began at Bemis Heights, near Saratoga, New York. When Arnold saw that the second American charge against the British was turning into a rout, he borrowed a horse, rallied the retreating troops, and led them on a heroic bayonet charge into the teeth of murderous British musket fire. Arnold's horse was shot out from under him at the end of the battle. Both the musket ball and the fall shattered his left leg. A controversial decision to set the bone rather than amputate left Arnold with a left leg that was two inches shorter than his right one.

Arnold escaped to the British, who gave him a general's commission and a cash bonus of £6,000. Although he commanded some British troops later in the Revolution, as a turncoat he was hardly welcomed with open arms. After the British withdrawal in 1783 Arnold left the United States, never to return.

So while it's true that Arnold was heroic, it is also important to remember his capacity for resentment, his thin skin, and his eye for a way to make a buck.

When he was being taken to the rear after his leg was shattered by that musket ball at Saratoga, Arnold is rumored to have remarked, "Better it had been in the chest." If he actually said it, he never said anything more correct during his entire life.

★ 8 ★

HORATIO GATES
The "Conway Cabal" and the Plot to "Get Rid" of George Washington
(CA. 1727–1806)

"Beware that your Northern laurels do not change
to Southern willows."
—General Charles Lee to General Horatio Gates after his victory at Saratoga

Ever wonder what might have happened to our country if George Washington got himself replaced as commander-in-chief of the Continental Army? Well it almost happened. And the bastard responsible was British-born Horatio Gates.

At first Gates hardly seemed like an opportunist. When the war broke out in 1775, the British Army veteran left his Virginia plantation. He offered his services to George Washington and was made made adjutant general of the Continental Army. As the top staff officer, Gates had made good use of his talents for organization and discipline learned during his twenty years in the British Army.

Two years later in 1777, British General John Burgoyne's entire army surrendered to Gates after the Battle of Saratoga. He simply took much of the credit owed his subordinate, Benedict Arnold, for their success against the British.

Where Gates was riding high, the fortunes of the Continental Army's Commander-in-Chief George Washington were at a low ebb. Washington lost popularity in Congress, having spent most of 1777 and 1778 fighting a series of losing battles all over New Jersey while trying to pry the British Army out of Philadelphia.

Gates saw the window of opportunity and leaped. He had his despicable aide James Wilkinson begin a whisper campaign suggesting that Washington had lost the confidence of both Congress and his own troops. The plot culminated with several letters written by an Irish-born French Army veteran officer named Thomas

Conway. Each complained about Washington's perceived shortcomings and implied that Gates stood ready to take over as an able commander-in-chief. The letters were forwarded to certain members of Congress to provoke a decision against Washington and for Gates. The Conway Cabal "plot," such as it was, didn't amount to much.

Conway resigned in disgrace once his letters and their contents were made public. One of Washington's staff officers challenged Conway to a duel, and shot him for his trouble. Conway survived to apologize to Washington and return to France.

There was one more moment in history when it looked as if Gates might succeed Washington. He had maneuvered his Congressional allies into naming him to Washington's staff by 1783, when hostilities with the British were largely over. The Continental Army was camped at Newburgh, New York, at the time, keeping an eye on the British in New York City. Restless and owed years of back pay, many of the officers of the army began to mutter about how they ought to march down to where Congress was in session and insist on receiving their pay. When Washington got wind of this, he made it clear that he would not allow the army to influence civilian political decisions in that manner.

At that point several of Gates's aides began to circulate more whispers among the disaffected officers. They pushed the notion that if Gates replaced Washington, the former would be open to airing their complaints much more forcibly with the Congress. And thus the so-called "Newburgh Conspiracy" was born.

In the end the Newburgh Conspiracy had no more success than the Conway Cabal did. Washington crashed a meeting chaired by Gates, gave his celebrated "Newburgh Address," which moved most of those assembled to tears, and effectively broke up the plot before it had a chance to gain any traction among the troops. And as a result the republic was spared a military coup at the beginning of its existence.

Horatio Gates: bastard.

★9★
ALEXANDER HAMILTON
The Bastard on the Ten-Dollar Bill
(CA. 1755–1804)

> "Hamilton is really a colossus . . . without numbers,
> he is a host unto himself."
> —Thomas Jefferson

History is rife with examples of intelligent, able government servants brought low by scandals in their private lives. In the case of Alexander Hamilton, a brief scandal in his personal life likely cost him the presidency.

By the age of twenty Hamilton was serving as General George Washington's aide de camp with the rank of colonel in the Continental Army. By the age of thirty he was helping found New York's first bank. He was one of the driving personalities behind the Constitutional Convention, and served as America's first secretary of the treasury, both before he turned thirty-five. The "bastard from Nevis" was a classic overachiever.

Like most overachievers, Hamilton was constantly courting favorable attention from those around him. This was particularly true where attractive women were concerned. Happily married with four children, Hamilton was thirty-six and the second-most powerful man in the country when he first encountered a prostitute named Maria Reynolds in 1791.

Married to a con man and pimp named James Reynolds, Reynolds sought out Hamilton at his Philadelphia home with quite a story. She had contacted Hamilton, she said, because he was a fellow New Yorker who might assist her. Maria said she was in desperate straits after her louse of a husband abandoned her.

Because she was a *young, beautiful* fellow New Yorker, Hamilton listened. He agreed to help and sent her back to her boarding house, having agreed to help her. Later that same day he took her some money. In his own words, "Some conversation ensued from which it was quickly apparent that other than pecuniary compensation would be acceptable." Luckily for us, Hamilton wrote an extensive account of his trysts with this young woman in a remarkable pamphlet with a longwinded title; today it's known widely as the "Reynolds Pamphlet."

For the next year Hamilton carried on with Maria Reynolds. Her husband likely had a hand in planning the whole thing and quickly began blackmailing Hamilton. It was only a matter of time before the whole thing came out.

A BORN BASTARD

Born poor and illegitimate in 1755 on tiny Nevis Island in the West Indies, Hamilton personified the "Great American Success Story." He always felt the need to prove himself, so he reinforced his brilliance with industry. His neighbors were so impressed that they took up a collection in order to send the eighteen-year-old assistant clerk to New York for a proper education. He left the West Indies in 1773, just in time to get involved in "the troubles" that later grew into the American Revolution.

When James Reynolds got caught in an unrelated swindle, he offered to give up a much bigger criminal if spared jail time. Of course, Hamilton was Reynolds's get-out-of-jail-free card. The resulting scandal quickly came to the attention of Democratic Republican Party boss (and future president) James Monroe. Monroe was a political rival of Hamilton's, so he approached Hamilton about his affair. Hamilton admitted it all while flatly denying any professional or political wrongdoing.

Monroe believed him, agreed not to make the matter public, and suggested Hamilton end things.

Hamilton did so. This was in 1792. Within a year Maria Reynolds had successfully sued for divorce from her husband; James Reynolds subsequently disappears from history. Hamilton resigned from Washington's government in 1795, and resumed his law practice in New York City.

Hamilton's publication of the Reynolds Pamphlet was his final attempt to "clear the air" on his affair. It blew up in his face. He never held political office again and died in an 1804 duel—that had nothing to do with the Reynolds affair—with Maria Reynolds's divorce lawyer (and fellow bastard) Aaron Burr.

★ 10 ★
JOHN RUTLEDGE
JWI (Judging While Insane)
(1739–1800)

> "The Rutledges have been at their wits end how to conduct them-
> selves in the delicate state of John's affairs."
> —Anonymous South Carolina politician

John Rutledge sacrificed much for his country during its infancy. He was a Revolutionary War hero; the scion of a distinguished South Carolina family; a distinguished
judge; a Founding Father; and one of the framers of the United States Constitution.
Today, however, we're not likely to remember him for his contributions. Rather he's
most likely to be remembered because he was kicked off the U.S. Supreme Court
for being crazy.

Rutledge was a successful lawyer when the American Revolution broke out. He
was so highly esteemed in his native South Carolina that he served as its "president"
under an interim constitution and then as its first governor once a more permanent
state constitution was in place. Rutledge even led the resistance against the British
invasion in 1780. He helped oversee the defense of Charleston Harbor and organized the city's evacuation once it fell into British hands. British soldiers destroyed
much of Rutledge's property during the resulting occupation; he was never fully
compensated for that loss.

Rutledge's political successes and personal losses continued to pile up even
after the Revolution ended. He signed the U.S. Constitution and served as chief
justice of the South Carolina Court of Common Pleas and Sessions. But during
the ensuing years Rutledge attempted unsuccessfully to recoup the financial losses
he'd suffered during the Revolution. In 1792 his wife died. The blow to Rutledge,
combined with the strain of trying to right his family's finances, pushed him to

the brink emotionally. Clearly suffering from what we recognize today as clinical depression, Rutledge's behavior became by turns manic and morose.

In spite of the whispers about Rutledge's increasingly erratic behavior, he still enjoyed a formidable reputation as one of the country's leading jurists. President Washington selected Rutledge to succeed John Jay as chief justice when Jay was elected governor of New York in 1795. Because the Senate was in recess as the change was made, they were denied the opportunity to assess the validity of rumors about Rutledge's mental state before he was confirmed. Their decision would have to wait until the Senate reconvened. Rutledge took the oath of office as chief justice on July 1, 1795, rumors of his stability be damned.

Rutledge's appointment to the Supreme Court had an immediate and unforgettable impact. Before leaving the Supreme Court, John Jay had negotiated a treaty with the British as a follow-up to the one that ended the American Revolution in 1783. The "Jay Treaty" ignored issues that the Southern states considered delicate and vital. Many statesmen expressed their dissent with the terms of the treaty, but Rutledge went nuts over it.

In what one historian later famously called "an unfortunate display of oratorical excess," Rutledge brutally condemned the treaty in a speech in Charleston soon after his appointment. At one point he even said "that he had rather the President should die than sign that puerile instrument." Later in the same speech Rutledge made it clear that he "preferred war to adoption of it." He gave his critics all of the ammunition they needed to add to Rutledge's growing list of faults. Rampant speculation that Rutledge had been drunk when he made the speech began soon afterwards, making public the fact that he was often "in his cups."

Rutledge's speech rocked the boat so badly that it wrecked his chances of Senate confirmation. No one in their right mind would approve of a chief justice who ranted so carelessly, much less one that did it drunk. On December 15, the Senate voted to reject Rutledge's appointment.

A full-blown nervous breakdown and a January suicide attempt by drowning followed. Rutledge was never the same after the Senate rejected his nomination. He died in 1800, a thoroughly depressed and broken man. He is the only chief justice of the United States to be removed from office for any reason.

★ 11 ★
WILLIAM BLOUNT
Trying to Sell the Southwest to the Spanish
(1749–1800)

> "I was much embarrassed between my regard for Governor Blount and what might possibly be my duty with respect to the letter."
> —James Carey after receiving proof of William Blount's bastardry

Did you know that one of the signers of the United States Constitution was actually the first United States Senator to be expelled from the Senate? It's true! The name of the rogue who won this dubious honor for even more dubious behavior? William Blount.

Blount was born in 1749 and raised in North Carolina. A trained lawyer, he served as a paymaster for various units of the state militia and the Continental Army. He never saw combat, but he earned the status (and the paycheck) of an officer.

Blount went on to represent North Carolina at the Constitutional Convention from 1787 to 1788. He was one of three delegates from North Carolina to sign the completed document. Before the ink was dry on the Constitution Blount had pulled up stakes and quit North Carolina for Tennessee. In 1790 President Washington appointed him governor of the new "Southwest Territory." The new job gave him control of a sparsely settled, booming region that included parts of what are now the states of Kentucky, Tennessee, Alabama, and Mississippi.

While serving as its governor, Blount found that the territory treated him well. He moved the territorial capital to Knoxville and began building himself a mansion there. Like everyone else with any money to invest in the West during this period, Blount was making a fortune off of land speculation, and the mansion he built reflected his growing wealth. Blount's popularity grew with the territory.

When Tennessee became a state in 1796 Blount chaired its constitutional convention. The state legislature promptly elected William Blount as one of its first U.S. Senators.

Even Blount didn't lead a truly charmed life, though. Within a year, rumors of war with either the French or the British caused land futures in the West to tumble, and Blount lost nearly his entire fortune.

So Blount schemed with the British. He offered the use of the contacts he had made with certain Indian tribes while serving as the Southwest Territory's Indian Agent. The plan: get the Indians to rise up and help the British conquer Florida, driving the Spanish out entirely. If the plan was successful, Florida would become a British colony, with William Blount as its first (very well-paid) colonial governor. Apparently he preferred working as a governor to working as a senator.

You can guess what happened next. Before anything could be made of the plan, a letter Blount wrote outlining it came into the possession of President John Adams.

Adams wasted no time turning the incriminating letter over to the Senate, and Blount had another big problem. As it turns out, not only is it against the law for American citizens to operate as agents of a foreign power, stirring up a convenient war on that foreign power's behalf is also illegal.

BASTARD BY ASSOCIATION?

One of William Blount's political protégés was future U.S. President Andrew Jackson. In fact Blount tried to bring Jackson into his scheme to turn Florida over to the British!

So on July 7, 1797, just four days after Adams turned over the letter in question, the House of Representatives voted to impeach Senator Blount. The Senate voted 25 to 1 (and you can just guess who cast that single "no" vote!) to expel Blount on the very next day. Surprisingly, expulsion from the Senate was pretty much the extent of Blount's punishment. He wasn't even impeached, let alone put on trial for treason. The Senate began impeachment deliberations but never completed them after having determined that all they were truly empowered to do was expel him from the Senate.

Instead Blount went back to Tennessee, where in 1798 he ran for and won a seat in the Tennessee State Senate. Within a year he was the speaker of the Senate (maybe he actually preferred senatorial hours after all?). Just a year after that, he died of natural causes in Knoxville, never having spent a day in jail.

★12★

JAMES WILSON

Swindler, Yazoo Land Scammer, U.S. Supreme Court Justice

(1742–1798)

"Without liberty, law loses its nature and its name, and becomes oppression. Without law, liberty also loses its nature and its name, and becomes licentiousness."
—James Wilson

James Wilson was a Scots-born lawyer; a judge; a Founding Father; a signer of the Declaration of Independence; and for a decade, one of the first Supreme Court Justices. But James Wilson was also a con man, a rascal, and an out-and-out thief largely responsible for the first post-colonial land-grab scandal in American history.

One of the new nation's first scoundrels, Wilson's list of dastardly deeds stretches back into the late colonial period. As a lawyer practicing in Philadelphia, he defended a number of loyalist landholders trying to recover property confiscated by the new Patriot government. Needless to say, he was no one's favorite. Wilson was so widely detested that a group of Pennsylvania militiamen actually fired a cannon at his home!

Like many of his fellow Americans, Wilson constantly speculated in frontier land. And like many other bastards, when he couldn't turn a profit, he spun a tale instead. He once fraudulently petitioned Congress for reimbursement for land he had supposedly bought from Indians in the Old Northwest Territory. In reality, he hadn't paid out a nickel. But Wilson's biggest money-grab by far was the one known as the Yazoo Land Scandal.

The Yazoo Strip was a section of the Old Southwest that bordered Georgia, the Carolinas, and Spanish Florida. Named for the Yazoo River that formed part of its western border, the strip was part of what would become Alabama and Mississippi and included ancestral lands of the Creek Indians. In the late 1790s, the Yazoo Strip was worth $10 million on the land market (equivalent to over $124.5 million today). To Wilson, though, it had even more potential.

In 1794 the state of Georgia owned much of the land to its west, including the Yazoo Strip. Wilson convinced Governor George Matthews that a land sale would bring in money *and* another term for the politically ambitious Matthews. In turn the governor persuaded the Georgia legislature to sell 40 million acres of Georgia's Yazoo lands to four different private land companies for the low, low price of $500,000. In retrospect, it's not at all surprising that Wilson had ties with each company in the deal. And as it turned out, several of the Georgia state legislators involved in the passage of the bill selling the land were bribed with stock in the companies buying the land. Talk about cutting out the middleman!

Wilson's bold move didn't go unnoticed. The details of the deal were made public and Matthews lost his bid for reelection in the aftermath. Georgia wound up repealing the bill calling for the sale and rendering the deeds to the lands in question worthless. The state then bought back much of the land that in turn had been sold by the land companies to other investors, after which Georgia ceded all of its land claims west of its current borders to the federal government.

When some of the investors who bought their parcels from the fraudulent land companies refused to sell their properties back to either the state or federal governments, the whole thing wound up in court. It eventually reached the U.S. Supreme Court, where the land sales (aside from the initial ones to the land companies that were bribing state officials) were deemed valid. The few people who bought titles to Yazoo land and stubbornly refused to sell did get their acreage for a song. But Wilson wasn't one of them.

He didn't really profit from even this far-ranging scheme. By the mid-1790s he owed so much money to so many people whom he had defrauded in one way or another that this serving U.S. Supreme Court Justice decided to work "on the run" as a circuit court judge (Supreme Court Justices did this until well into the nineteenth century). In Wilson's case he served continually for years, never staying in one place long enough for his creditors to catch up with him. He died broke and still running, in 1798.

★13★
JOHN ADAMS
"His Rotundity" and the Alien & Sedition Acts
(1737–1826)

> "Because power corrupts, society's demands for moral authority and character increase as the importance of the position increases."
> —John Adams

John Adams was a truly impressive man. A guiding light of the American Revolution and one of the intellectual forces behind the Declaration of Independence. He was the second president of the United States and founder (along with his beloved wife Abigail) of the Adams family dynasty.

Adams was also thin-skinned, ill tempered, abrupt, given to bouts of depression and not above bullying anyone in order to get his way. And he used the law in a ham-handed attempt to bypass Constitutional rights in the name of security and power.

After all, the American Revolution had ended barely fifteen years before Adams took office and more strife was brewing. A continent-wide war threatened to tear through Europe in the wake of the French Revolution, and the British and French were mainly to blame. During Adams's presidency, the United States struggled to maintain neutrality between its European business interests, and from 1797 to 1801 the United S attempted to trade with both countries.

But Americans repeatedly found themselves pushed to take sides in the fray. Both of these nations seized American ships carrying cargoes for their enemies. The United States called for both sides to respect its neutrality rights, but to no avail. Things got so bad that the United States rebuilt its decommissioned navy and fought an undeclared naval "Quasi-War" with France from 1797 to 1799.

Inside the United States, pro-British and pro-French sympathies pitted the American public against itself. Many worried that a civil war would start over European discord. Adams and his Federalist Party hurried to assert control. With Adams's blessing, Congress passed four laws known collectively as the Alien and Sedition Acts in an early attempt to head off trouble. These laws empowered the president to deport any noncitizen who showed too much sympathy to a foreign country. They also made it tougher for foreigners to become citizens and made it a crime to publish anything derogatory about any federal employee, from the president on down.

WHAT'S IN A (NICK)NAME?

Adams had a love of both good food and fine clothes. Given his incipient pomposity, these traits served to set Adams up for his fair share of ridicule. His predecessor George Washington was an impressive physical specimen who at 6′4″ towered over most men of his day and had been addressed as "His Excellency the President." In comparison, Adams's short, stockier figure lent itself to him being referred to as "His Rotundity the President" both in print and behind his back.

Adams's support of the Sedition Act was particularly ironic. The British government passed several similar laws in the 1760s, and Adams had fought them as a younger man. Both acts also directly violated the First Amendment. The crackdown on free speech was intended to stifle dissent among those who opposed the Federalists. Vice President Thomas Jefferson and his new Democratic Republican party had often been strongly, even brutally critical of Adams in the press.

But the new laws failed to completely silence Jefferson and his followers. Instead they simply found new, less direct means of slamming Adams and the Federalists.

In the end the move was a flat failure.

Although Adams never actually deported anyone, many foreign citizens got the point and left the country. Adams rarely had opposition newspaper editors jailed, but in the public eye the damage was done. Many Americans viewed his actions as a dangerous precedent barring free speech. In 1800 public distrust helped make

Adams a one-term president. The people elected Adams's former friend and Vice President Jefferson in his place.

Adams left town the night before rather than attend Jefferson's inauguration. Later in life the two would rekindle their remarkable friendship, but at the time John Adams's inherent pettiness made that impossible.

"I should be deficient in candor, were I to conceal the conviction, that [Adams] does not possess the talents adapted to the administration of Government, and that there are great and intrinsic defects in his character, which unfit him for the office of Chief Magistrate."

—Alexander Hamilton

★14★
THOMAS JEFFERSON
The Slave Who Bore His Children
(1743–1826)

> "We hold these truths to be self-evident; that all men
> are created equal."
> —Thomas Jefferson

Thomas Jefferson penned some of the most famous words about equality and freedom in American history. The same man owned slaves, inherited slaves from his father and his father-in-law, and left slaves to his heirs in his will. But the hypocrisy of Thomas Jefferson, great American politician, philosopher, and scientist, does not end there. In keeping with established custom in eighteenth century America, Jefferson took a slave concubine and had children by her. By our modern standards, that qualifies him as something of a bastard to say the least.

Jefferson married young, but became a young widower. His wife Martha died in her early thirties after giving birth to six children, only two of whom survived infancy. On her deathbed Martha begged Jefferson to swear that he would never remarry. He gave her his word he wouldn't. And he never did.

But in Virginia at the time it was not uncommon for widowers to take up with slave women owned by them. In fact, Jefferson's own father-in-law had done so.

One of the results of that union was a slave girl named Sally Hemings. When Jefferson's father-in-law died, Sally, her many siblings, and her mother all became Jefferson's property.

Sally was three-quarters white (her mother had been half white), but because of the law at the time, children of slaves took their legal status from their mothers: if the mothers were slaves, so were the children, and they too became the property of their mother's master.

Sally Hemings had at least six children (there were possibly more). None of the Hemings family worked as field hands on Jefferson's plantation, but none of them were ever freed during Jefferson's lifetime. He ensured that all of Sally's children were educated and taught a variety of skills; several of the children even played the violin as he did. Still others learned carpentry, spinning, and other trades that could support them once they were no longer his slaves. Does Jefferson's apparent involvement in their lives explain why he never freed Sally or any of their children during his lifetime?

LE BATARD?

By the time Jefferson and his family returned from France and resumed residence on his estate at Monticello, he had likely begun his affair with Sally. Much has been made of the fact that slavery was illegal while she lived in France, and she could have petitioned for her freedom and didn't. For some this is a measure of the fact that she returned Jefferson's affections. Whether she did or didn't care about Jefferson, she didn't have much in the way of options other than submitting to his advances. A female, emancipated, multiracial, foreign, ex-slave had even fewer choices in life than a female slave did in 1790s Revolutionary France.

No. Jefferson freed Sally's children in his will, but he made no provision for Sally beyond willing her to his oldest daughter. It was up to Martha to free the mother of most of her half-siblings.

Perhaps Jefferson couldn't bear the thought of his daughter, her family, or the public finding out about his siring these children?

That's unlikely. Rumors about Jefferson siring the children of one of his slaves first emerged in print as early as 1802, and the whispers continued throughout his lifetime and afterward. Plus, the family resemblance between Jefferson and the children he had with Sally Hemings was remarkably strong. In the words of his own grandson Thomas Jefferson Randolph, Sally Hemings' children resembled Jefferson "so closely that it was plain that they had his blood in their veins."

Sally Hemings (and her children) never had a say, never had a choice, and never had real options, when it was within Jefferson's power to grant them. Call it callous, call it ignorant, but it is what makes our third president a bastard, "Great Man" or not.

★15★
JOHN PICKERING
JWI (Judging While Impaired)
(1737–1805)

> "The enclosed papers tended to show that Judge Pickering, owing to habits of intoxication or other causes, had become a scandal to the bench, and was unfit to perform his duties."
> —Henry Adams

America has had a long love-hate relationship with its judiciary. This is especially true of federal judges. Their rulings often impact the average American directly. We tend to either celebrate or detest our federal judges depending on whether or not we agree with their decisions. So when judges get caught having affairs or taking bribes, the public outrage ratchets up a notch. And when judges do something bad enough, it can even cost them their places on the bench.

IMPEACH THE BASTARDS!

Judges are rarely forced from the bench, but it does happen. In our country's history, only fourteen federal judges have had impeachment proceedings brought against them. Of those fourteen, only seven were convicted and removed from office. Four were acquitted, and three resigned before their trial in the Senate could take place.

Who was the first bastard on the short list of federal judges to lose his job? Ladies and gentlemen, we give you Judge John Pickering of New Hampshire.

Pickering was a Revolutionary War hero who also helped draft New Hampshire's state constitution. Over the course of his long career in state politics he served on the state supreme court and built a formidable reputation.

But by the time Washington appointed Pickering to the federal bench in 1795, he had also developed problems with overusing alcohol and under-using his sanity.

Over the course of the next eight years, Pickering showed up drunk for court numerous times. On a number of occasions he interrupted the proceedings by raving, swearing, tearing at his hair, and screaming at the top of his lungs. And this was when he showed up for court at all. His absenteeism from the bench was a more serious blow to his reputation as a jurist. But since a bastard's fate often boils down to politics, the real problem for Pickering turned out to be his party affiliation.

Pickering was a Federalist. His party initially controlled the U.S. federal court system, and packed it with party members before Thomas Jefferson and the Democratic Republicans took power in 1801. The new majority needed ways to get more of their own people appointed. A vague Constitutional clause outlined impeachment and the Jeffersonians were happy to have even a loosely legal way to get the job done.

Pickering made the battle easy for his opponents. By 1803, he stopped coming to court altogether, forcing his staff to request a replacement judge until he "recovered his health." Pickering was a Federalist, at least a habitual drunk, and quite likely deranged; the Democratic Republicans used these reasons to attempt to remove a sitting federal judge who had committed no actual crime. They wanted to be able to use "odd behavior" as an excuse for ridding the courts of as many Federalist judges as possible. Pickering's conviction and removal would set that precedent.

Pickering didn't do himself any favors when his Senate trial began in March 1803. As he had done so many times in his own courtroom, he failed to show up! His son came forward and pleaded to be allowed to present evidence that his father was insane and therefore not guilty (as if that would keep him from being removed from office!). The prosecution, made up of members of the House of Representatives, argued that Pickering was sane but drunk while presiding over court, an act which qualified as what the Constitution refers to as "high crimes and misdemeanors," conduct serious enough to justify removing a federal judge from office. The proceedings went back and forth along these lines for a week, but the outcome was a foregone conclusion.

On March 12, the Senate voted along party lines to convict and remove Pickering from his position as a federal judge, the first such case in American history. Pickering descended into full-on dementia afterward and died two years later.

SAMUEL CHASE
"Old Bacon Face"—an Unimpeachable Bastard
(1741–1811)

> "It is your lot to have the peculiar privilege of being universally despised."
> —Alexander Hamilton to Samuel Chase

Born in 1741, Samuel Chase was the only son of a Maryland minister and his wife. From these humble beginnings, he grew up to be one of the foremost lawyers of his community. Chase was also an early and ardent leader of colonial tax resistance during the 1760s and 1770s. A signatory of the Declaration of Independence, he also served as first a Maryland state judge and later as an associate justice of the U.S. Supreme Court.

And he was a bullying, war-profiteering bastard saddled with the nickname "Old Bacon Face" in part because of his irascible personality. Chase was even more anti-British than the most hardcore, true believer among the Sons of Liberty. Chase was elected to both the first and second Continental Congresses, and he kept himself busy twisting arms to ensure Maryland's legislature voted for liberty. He also tried to peel Britain's Canadian colonies away by luring them into the Patriot confederation.

Chase possessed a first class intellect and a fine legal mind, but he was likely the most difficult man to get along with in the Congress. He made hair shirts like John Adams seem pleasant by comparison. So while his ability and passion made him indispensable, his personality made him unpopular.

On top of that, he was a greedy bastard. He schemed to corner the bread market in the colonies during the first years of the war. When a Philadelphia newspaper broke this news in 1778, Chase resigned in disgrace from Congress.

Within a few years he was back in the thick of things, though. Appointed a Maryland judge after the Revolution, he served with such fortitude that President Washington named him to the U.S. Supreme Court in 1796.

Chase's bad temper, bullying ways, and tendency to mouth off from the bench got him in fresh trouble once he took his seat on the Supreme Court. When Thomas Jefferson and his Democratic Republicans started culling their opponents from the courts, they also resolved to remove Chase from office. But in setting their sights on Chase, the Democratic Republicans chose one of the most competent jurists of the era. And Samuel Chase was determined not to be the next John Pickering.

STAMP ACT BASTARD

During the Stamp Act Crisis, the colonists protested British taxation levied in the form of government-issued stamps. Twenty-four-year-old Chase led the Annapolis branch of the Sons of Liberty in a smash-and-grab at the offices of the local printer who contracted with the British to make their stamps. Chase himself then burned the local tax collector in effigy, along with all of the stamps his gang had collected. That might have been enough to satisfy most Patriot hotheads; the fire-breathing Chase, however, wanted more. When Annapolis's mayor denounced Chase in one of the local newspapers, Chase boldly responded. Dismissing the mayor and other Maryland loyalists as nothing but "despicable tools of power," Chase openly boasted about the break-in.

Chase proved he was a superb lawyer in part by showing the good sense to hire other lawyers to defend him. He was acquitted and quickly proved that the Jeffersonian impeachment strategy wouldn't serve to pack their cronies into the federal courts. Even if the judges they targeted weren't good lawyers like Chase, they likely knew a couple they wouldn't be afraid to employ.

Great strategy. Still a bastard.

★17★
JAMES WILKINSON
A New and Improved Benedict Arnold
(1755–1825)

"The most finished scoundrel that ever lived."
—John Randolph

Everyone has heard of Benedict Arnold and Aaron Burr, neither of whom was very successful in his treasonous endeavors. But there were successful ones, too, villains like America's greatest traitor James Wilkinson. Wilkinson was born to a wealthy Maryland family in 1755 and was studying medicine in Philadelphia when the Revolution broke out. He eagerly set aside his studies and enlisted for service in the Continental Army. He took part in Washington's encirclement of Boston, and served as a staff officer with Arnold at the Siege of Quebec. He even jumped to General Gates's staff in time to take part in the victory at Saratoga in 1777.

Wilkinson, however, also took part in the Conway Cabal against George Washington, which did nothing to endear him to his army superiors. Within a year even Gates had gotten fed up with Wilkinson and forced him to resign his commission. Wilkinson returned to active service as a supply officer in 1779. He was again forced to resign again, this time in the face of charges of corruption. It was the first of many times he would fight such allegations.

Whatever his crimes in the army, Wilkinson had big plans for profit on the civilian front. In 1784 he met with the Louisiana Territory's Spanish governor, Esteban Rodriguez Miró. They plotted to seize a trade monopoly on the Mississippi River for Kentucky. Wilkinson took bribes from the Spanish and promised to help Kentucky declare its independence. He argued that an independent country of Kentucky could act as a buffer between Spanish colonies and the land-hungry United States. The citizens of Kentucky might even consent to union with the Spanish territories.

By the late 1790s Wilkinson was back in the army. This time he was a commissioned general stationed on the Southwestern frontier. Still a Spanish spy, he passed much information along to the Spanish regarding American aims on New Orleans.

It was years before any of this came to light. Seen as a loyal career officer, Wilkinson was eventually appointed Louisiana's first territorial governor. He ruled from New Orleans as a virtual military dictator. A number of prominent citizens complained about his methods to the national government. President Jefferson then ordered a full investigation of Wilkinson's conduct. Wilkinson, however, was more than prepared. He turned over information about the territorial ambitions of former Vice President Aaron Burr as a way of saving his own skin.

It worked. Burr went on trial for treason and Wilkinson testified against him. Wilkinson's testimony made such an impression that Virginia Democrat and prosecutor John Randolph said, "Wilkinson is the only man I ever saw who is from the bark to the very core a villain!"

Wilkinson served without distinction in the War of 1812 and then retired to write his memoirs (which should have been shelved in the "fiction" section). He died in Mexico in 1825, hoping to make a fortune bringing American settlers into the sparsely populated Texas region.

It is fitting that one of America's most successful traitors died and was buried outside of the country. It is especially ironic in light of the fact that Wilkinson was never caught in his lifetime. His involvement with the Spanish did not surface until the 1850s, when his letters to the Spanish governor in New Orleans were published.

This is, of course, why Wilkinson was more successful than any other traitor on an enemy payroll. When James Wilkinson died in Mexico at age seventy, he had been suspected of all manner of corruption. But no one in the government or outside of it suspected his long association (for pay) with the Spanish. That is the very definition of a successful spy, and one of the definitions of an outright bastard.

"[Wilkinson was] a general who never won a battle or lost a court-martial."
—**Robert Leckie, historian**

AARON BURR
Successful Duelist and Failed Secessionist
(1756–1836)

"Burr is sanguine enough to hope everything—daring enough to attempt everything—wicked enough to scruple nothing."
—Alexander Hamilton

In 1800 Thomas Jefferson won the presidency by the thinnest of margins in a vote that had to be settled in the House of Representatives. He almost lost the presidency to a brilliant, restless polymath named Aaron Burr, who became vice president according to electoral law at the time. Before the end of Jefferson's second term Burr would stand trial for treason; he was the only member of the U.S. executive branch to ever do so.

Burr was born in New Jersey in 1756, the grandson of the great Puritan minister Jonathan Edwards. His legal studies were interrupted by the outbreak of the American Revolution. Like many he volunteered for service with the Continental Army. By the end of the Revolution, Burr had distinguished himself by rising to the rank of colonel. He held a number of political offices in short order, then in a senatorial election 1791 he defeated one of New York's incumbent senators Phillip Schuyler. Burr and Schuyler's son-in-law Alexander Hamilton had been friends up to that point, but after the election became bitter enemies.

Their falling-out helps explain Hamilton's public support for Jefferson during the election of 1800. In Hamilton's view, Jefferson placed the public good before his own interests. He saw Burr, on the other hand, as a dangerous opportunist who placed his own interests before anyone else's.

Burr eventually grew bored by the vice presidency, and in 1804 he decided to run for governor of New York. Shortly afterward Hamilton made some cutting remarks about Burr's character. Burr then challenged his former friend to a duel.

The two fought in Weehawken, New Jersey, and Hamilton was killed. Burr faced murder charges in both New York and New Jersey for a time. The allegations forced him to hide out while the hullabaloo over Hamilton's death blew over. Eventually the charges were dropped, and Burr went back to his normal routine.

When Burr's term of office as vice president ended in 1805, he headed west. He had leased 40,000 acres of land in Texas, and claimed that he planned to build on that initial piece of land.

The truth wasn't so simple.

Burr's plan did include building, but he also intended to "filibuster" (lead a private military expedition) into Mexico. Though his design was illegal, it may not have actually been treasonous. And he might have managed to take the land he wanted had he not told so many people the secret. Burr had traveled far and wide, mentioning different bits of the plan to a host of people, many of whom he hoped to involve in his plot (including a Tennessee militia general named Andrew Jackson).

So when James Wilkinson claimed that Burr in fact intended to also peel off a number of the Western states in the Union and produced letters written by Burr to that effect, the accusation didn't seem unfounded. Burr once again found himself in hot water. Just as he had done after he killed Hamilton, Burr went to ground. This time, however, a federal arrest warrant issued by President Jefferson himself caught up with Burr, and he was arrested in what is now Alabama.

Burr was charged with treason in a federal court in Virginia in 1807 and faced death for his intended crimes. President Jefferson had publicly declared that Burr was guilty, thereby attaching the president's personal prestige to the widely held belief in Burr's guilt. But the evidence against Burr was largely circumstantial, and his lawyers destroyed Wilkinson's credibility as a witness. Once again found not guilty, he walked.

Burr spent most of the rest of his years roaming the world, a restless spirit for the remainder of his long life, fleeing creditors and chasing opportunity. At age seventy-seven he married a wealthy widow whose inheritance he quickly ran through, just as he had any money that had ever come into his hands. Burr died, on the day his divorce from his second wife became final, aged eighty, a bastard to the end.

★19★
THE FEDERALISTS
The Hartford Convention and the Lousy Timing of Treason
(1814)

Secession movements don't play well in this country. Just look at what happened to the Southern gentlemen who voted to secede from the Union in 1860 and 1861. The national government fought a long and bloody war in which more Americans died than in all of the other wars in which Americans have served and fought *combined*.

And to think, that civil war could well have been fought four decades earlier, beginning in 1814, if the pack of bastards who convened the infamous "Hartford Convention" had gotten their way. Here's what happened.

In 1800 Thomas Jefferson and the Democratic Republicans swept the Federalist Party from power. The Federalists lost both the White House and Congress to their mostly Southern and Western rivals. At the same time, the United States was fighting to prosper as the Napoleonic Wars raged across Europe. Both the British and the French had violated American neutrality time and time again. As soon as he was in office, Jefferson began to retaliate against both sides of this conflict with a trade embargo of all European goods. The United States, he said, would prosecute an "economic war" and deny the British and the French one of their largest emerging markets.

Since shipping and shipbuilding were New England's largest industries, the embargo was an unqualified disaster for the region. As a result the state governments of all five New England states were soon solidly Federalist. Jefferson's successor James Madison stepped into office in 1809. He extended Jefferson's economic policies so far as that he actually started the War of 1812 with Britain over the issue. He also curtailed the defensive abilities of New England's state governments. These five troubled states were seen by most of the rest of the country (especially the South) as being potentially disloyal.

Turns out the rest of the country was right.

By late 1814, New England's economy was in shambles, and no end to the war was in sight. A group of prominent Federalists led by Harrison Gray Otis called for a convention of delegates representing all five New England states to meet in secret in Hartford, Connecticut, in December 1814.

BASTARD PROPOSAL

The delegates wrote up a proposal that called for the national government to pass the following constitutional amendments:

1. Limit all embargoes to less than sixty days.
2. Revoke the Southern right to count slaves as three-fifths of citizen for the purpose of determining representation in the Congress.
3. Limit future presidents to a single term.
4. Require a two-thirds Congressional majority for declaration of war, disruption of foreign trade, or admitting a new state to the Union.
5. Bar incoming presidents from being from the same state as their immediate predecessors (All of the presidents to that point, with the brief intermission of John Adams's administration from 1797–1801, had been Virginians. This was intended to end the so-called "Virginia Dynasty").

There was no way that the Republican-controlled Congress would have passed any of the amendments the Convention advocated. This proposal was only intended to be a bargaining chip to get the rest of the country to take New England seriously. The New Englanders wanted other states to negotiate with their state governments, as opposed to continuing to ignore their collective concerns.

A month later the Hartford Convention adjourned and sent representatives to Washington, D.C. By this time, word of Andrew Jackson's victory at New Orleans, and the signing of the treaty that ended the war, had reached the District of Columbia.

Could their timing have been worse?

The Hartford Convention finished what the election of 1800 had started and signaled the death (by suicide) of the Federalist Party. After the brief honeymoon of the Era of Good Feeling, sectionalism in America would return with a vengeance. Over the next forty-five years internal bickering would help drag the country spiraling into the Civil War so narrowly avoided in 1815.

The Federalists: proof that if you can be a bastard, "Timing" can be a bitch!

★ 20 ★
HENRY CLAY
The "Corrupt Bargain" and the Election of 1824
(1777–1852)

"I'd rather be right than president."
—Henry Clay

If ever Kentuckian Henry Clay told a lie, it was in the above quote. The man wanted to be president with every fiber of his being. Charismatic, shrewd, several times U.S. Senator and Speaker of the House of Representatives, Clay spent decades seeking the Oval Office, running for president three different times, the first time in 1824.

By 1824 President James Monroe was facing retirement. He had no like-minded Virginia aristocrat serving as his secretary of state and positioned to continue the "Virginia Dynasty." The unnerving (for other states, especially in New England) and steady flow of Virginians through the executive branch began with Thomas Jefferson, was carried on by James Madison, and seemed destined to end with Monroe himself. Thus the election of 1824 promised to be the most open one so far in the short history of the young republic.

This is not to say that Monroe's actual secretary of state did not harbor presidential ambitions or that he wasn't capable. In many ways John Quincy Adams, who had entered public life while in his teens, was the ablest secretary of state that America has ever produced.

But Adams lacked the "common touch." In 1824, ever more liberal voter registration laws were allowing more and more of the "unwashed masses"—in other words, the poor—to vote. The common touch was becoming a political necessity. And no politician in the United States typified the "everyman" more than former militia general, Indian fighter, frontier judge, and U.S. Senator Andrew Jackson of Tennessee. As if these two larger-than-life statesmen weren't enough, there were several other candidates for the presidency in that year of change; among them was Henry Clay.

The ensuing campaign was remarkable for its viciousness. Not since the election of 1800 when the elder Adams lost to Jefferson had the nation seen such vitriol spewed between competing political camps.

Jackson easily won a majority of the popular vote, but he failed to gain a majority of either states or electoral votes. The deadlock passed the election decision to the House of Representatives for a tiebreaker vote. And Henry Clay was Speaker of the House.

WHY THE BASTARD DID IT

Clay and Adams had known and disliked each other for over a decade, having worked closely together as members of the American peace delegation that negotiated the end of the War of 1812 in Ghent, Belgium. But if Clay disliked Adams, he despised Jackson and feared the Tennessean's appeal to the "mob." Clay had decided long before the House convened to settle the election question in 1825 that he was going to throw his support behind Adams; the question was what he would receive in return. The answer: he would be secretary of state, a position considered—at the time—to be the stepping-stone to the presidency.

Clay and Adams claimed that although they met several times before the House vote, no promises were made and no favors done. But shortly after Clay swung the votes to ensure Adams's victory, Adams announced that he intended to make Clay his secretary of state. Since every president from Jefferson onward to the younger Adams had served as secretary of state, Adams had essentially acknowledged Clay as his political heir.

It did Clay no good in the end. Jackson ran again in 1828 and cleaned Adams's clock. Clay would go on to continue a distinguished career in the Senate and earn the nickname "The Great Compromiser." But he would never get closer to the presidency than he had in 1824 when he sold out Andrew Jackson.

"The Judas of the West has closed the contract and will receive the thirty pieces of silver. . . . Was there ever witnessed such a bare faced corruption in any country before?"
—Andrew Jackson on Henry Clay and the "corrupt bargain" of 1824

★21★

KING MOB
The Inauguration Day Trashing
of the White House
(1829)

"The reign of KING MOB seemed triumphant."
—Joseph Story

March 4, 1829: a sixty-two-year-old veteran prepared for a day history would never forget. His career had been flush with success and honor. He served in several wars, including the American Revolution; was appointed the first governor of Florida; was elected first congressman from Tennessee; spent two-terms as a United States senator; and commanded the victorious American troops at the historic Battle of New Orleans. That late winter morning, he strode down Pennsylvania Avenue hatless, clad in a black suit and string tie to honor his recently deceased wife. President-Elect Andrew Jackson had a date with destiny; it was his inauguration day.

Jackson and many of his supporters viewed that day as long overdue. After he won the election of 1828 in a landslide vote and handily defeating incumbent John Quincy Adams and a field of other challengers, Jackson had pledged that he would reform the federal government. He insisted that the common people would be represented, not just the monied interests and the same old political elites who acted as if political power and influence were theirs by birthright.

Jackson considered himself a man of the people, and the people seemed to love him for it. So in the weeks before Jackson's inauguration, the national capital had experienced a steady influx of visitors from all walks of life and every possible rung on the social ladder. All of them determined to bear witness to one of their own taking hold of the reins of on the West Portico of the Capitol Building. By the time that

Jackson took his long walk down Pennsylvania Avenue on that fateful March day, an immense, loud, colorful crowd had gathered to await him.

Although he was required to attend the inauguration because of his place on the high court, Supreme Court Justice Joseph Story left as quickly as he could in order to get away from the crowd. Jackson's predecessor John Quincy Adams followed the example of his own father twenty-eight years earlier and stayed away altogether. The District's fifteen federal marshals stretched a ship's cable across the Capitol's East Portico in an attempt to keep the crowd back.

Jackson took the oath of office and then addressed the throng. He spoke for only ten minutes, renewing his campaign promise to weed out political corruption in the national government. Then he returned to the White House. A long procession of his admirers followed, blocking Pennsylvania Avenue with the sheer weight of their numbers.

Breaking completely with previous precedent, Jackson had insisted that his new residence be open to the public on this day. Thousands of his fellow Americans took him up on the invitation.

Washington socialite and novelist Margaret Bayard Smith later wrote of the celebration:

> *What a scene did we witness! The Majesty of the People had disappeared, and a rabble, a mob, of boys, negros, women, children, scrambling, fighting, romping. What a pity, what a pity.*

By the end of the day the entire first floor of the White House was a complete wreck. Jackson himself quietly left by a set of back stairs and spent the night in the rooming house he'd rented upon entering the city the previous week. Those revelers left behind were only coaxed out of the White House by the quick thinking of its staff: they removed the punch bowls (filled with more liquor than "punch") from the building and set them up out on the South Lawn.

Along with Jackson and everything and everyone he represented, Democracy (after a fashion) had arrived in the national capital on March 4, 1829. And on that day, as has often proven many times since, Democracy showed itself to be something of a bastard.

★22★
ANDREW JACKSON
"King Andrew I"
(1767–1845)

"Do they think that I am such a damned fool as to think myself fit for President of the United States? No, sir; I know what I am fit for. I can command a body of men in a rough way, but I am not fit for President."
—Andrew Jackson, 1821

Former national and frontier politician, judge, militia general, Indian fighter, and hero of the Battle of New Orleans, Andrew Jackson began serving his country as a teenager during the American Revolution. Orphaned, marked by smallpox, and scarred across the face by the slash of a British officer's sword after Jackson—a prisoner at the time—refused to polish that officer's boots Jackson's service left him diamond hard.

So tough that his troops had nicknamed him "Old Hickory," Jackson was intelligent, ruthless, stubborn, determined, and—when he chose to be—charming. Many of the common folk in the country found him and his appealing "rags to riches" life story irresistible. Thousands of them voted for him for president in 1824, when he got more votes than any other candidate but still lost the presidency. Jackson won the election of 1828 and served as president for eight stormy years from 1829–1837.

During that presidency Jackson proved himself to be quite a bastard. Among other things, he took it on himself to destroy the banking system (with help from Martin Van Buren). He also dispossessed most of the remaining Indian tribes east of the Mississippi. And through sheer force of will he shut down a crisis that threatened to break the country apart in civil war.

For his part, Jackson claimed that removing the Cherokees was "humane," moving them "out of the way" of encroaching white settlement. Some favor.

It was during the last of these crises (known as the "Nullification Crisis") that Jackson's outright bastardry might have been the single most likely thing holding the nation together. The affair pitted Jackson against several Southern states, including South Carolina, and Vice President John C. Calhoun, in a battle over federal tariffs. The president did not allow sectional sympathy to sway him during this crisis. He sent federal troops into the state in response to news that South Carolina's governor had raised a militia of 25,000.

WELL-INTENTIONED BASTARDRY?

The Cherokee Indians of northern Georgia assimilated so completely with their Caucasian neighbors that they became known as one of the so-called "Civilized Tribes." But when gold was discovered in their ancestral lands, Georgia sought to remove the Cherokees. The Cherokees took their case all the way to the U.S. Supreme Court, which ruled in their favor. It didn't matter. President Jackson didn't lift a finger to halt Cherokee removal. According to a quote made famous by time, Jackson supposedly said of the ruling, "(Chief Justice) Marshall has made his decision, now let him enforce it." But he didn't say that. What he really said merely acknowledged Georgia's stubbornness: "the decision of the Supreme Court has fell still born, and they find that they cannot coerce Georgia to yield to its mandate." The Cherokee Nation was forcibly removed from its ancestral lands in 1838. The route they followed westward into "Indian Territory" (now Oklahoma) became known in Cherokee as *nu-na-hi-du-na-tlo-hi-lu-i*, which means "the Trail Where They Cried." More than 4,000 of the 13,000 Cherokees who made the journey perished on the trail.

At the height of the tension, Jackson had a visitor who informed him that he was going to South Carolina for a visit, and asked whether the president had any message to pass along to his friends there. The president responded with characteristic bluntness:

"Please give my compliments to my friends in your State and say to them, that if a single drop of blood shall be shed there in opposition to the laws of the United States, I will hang the first man I can lay my hand on engaged in such treasonable conduct, upon the first tree I can reach."

South Carolina gave in.

Effective bastard.

JOHN C. CALHOUN
Secretary of War, Senator, Vice President, Traitor!
(1782–1850)

"The Government of the absolute majority instead of the Government of the people is but the Government of the strongest interests; and when not efficiently checked, it is the most tyrannical and oppressive that can be devised."
—John Calhoun

An able politician with a strong personality, John C. Calhoun wore many hats during his nearly fifty years of public service. He was a member of the House of Representatives; a longtime senator from South Carolina; a secretary of war for James Monroe; secretary of state for John Tyler; and vice president of the United States during the administrations of both John Quincy Adams and Andrew Jackson. Calhoun was also such a zealous advocate of states' rights that his beliefs led him to commit treason against the very government he had sworn to protect.

The Tariff of 1828 was a nationally divisive issue. President Jackson and his Northern allies supported the law. It protected fledgling Northern industries that were being driven out of business by a market flooded by cheaper British goods. The Southern states, however, called it the "Tariff of Abominations." The South had an agricultural economy, and its major trading partner was not the rapidly industrializing Northern states. Southern cotton most often sold to British, not American, buyers. Calhoun felt he couldn't turn his back on his fellow Southerners just to save face with the president. His vocal opposition put him in a politically awkward position.

Once the United States enacted the tariff, the British responded with heavy taxes on goods from the United States, including on Southern cotton. This in turn hurt

Southern exports as much as Jefferson's embargo had hurt New England's shipping industry twenty years before.

Calhoun could not silently bear what he considered an injustice to his native region. He penned *The South Carolina Exposition and Protest* as a condemnation of the tariff. Since he was still Jackson's vice president, Calhoun published his treatise anonymously. In the essay, Calhoun supported nullification. He used legal theory to suggest that a state ought to be able to "nullify" (or cancel out) a federal law within the boundaries of the state itself. The plan would have allowed the South to continue selling cotton to British mills without paying heavy taxes. And it would have allowed any state to throw out any federal law with which its citizens disagreed.

By actively advocating the circumvention of the U.S. Constitution, Calhoun committed treason. And like the organizers of the Hartford Convention before him, Calhoun paid a price for his perfidy. His actions in this case cost him any possibility of ever succeeding Andrew Jackson as president.

Calhoun was doubly unfortunate in his timing. By the time Jackson got word that Calhoun had secretly written the *Exposition*, he had also discovered that Calhoun had worked against him earlier in their careers. Calhoun had lobbied for Jackson to be court-martialed for dereliction of duty back in 1818, when Calhoun was Monroe's secretary of war, and Jackson and his militia were chasing British agents and Seminoles into Spanish-held Florida.

When Jackson asked him about this, Calhoun equivocated and made excuses. It didn't help that Calhoun had been scheming to fill the cabinet with his own political allies during the whole "Eaton Affair." This perfect storm of poorly timed and two-faced political choices resulted in a permanent break between the two men. Martin Van Buren of New York replaced Calhoun as vice president and Jackson's political heir; Calhoun went home to South Carolina to sulk.

Although he eventually partially rehabilitated his reputation, and returned to Washington as by turns secretary of state and U.S. Senator from his beloved South Carolina, Calhoun never again got close to the White House.

And the country was the better for it.

"That I didn't shoot Henry Clay and hang John C. Calhoun."
—Andrew Jackson when asked at the end of his life whether he had any regrets

★24★
JOHN AND PEGGY EATON
Washington's Original "Baby Daddy" Scandal
(1790–1856)

"Indeed the prejudice is so strong against [the Eatons] here, that Major Eaton has spoken of resigning and it seems the most proper course for him to pursue."
—Emily Donelson

When Andrew Jackson set about choosing the members of his cabinet, he included a few personal friends, among them his secretary of war, John H. Eaton. The two men had served together in the Senate, and Jackson, with no children of his own, took a fatherly interest in the much younger Eaton.

Rumor had it that Eaton was carrying on a years-long affair with Margaret "Peggy" O'Neill Timberlake. He was a handsome widower; she was the beautiful daughter of an Irish immigrant pub owner. But she was married. Her husband, a purser in the U.S. Navy, had money troubles and was often away on long voyages. Eaton had befriended the couple before Timberlake's circumstances forced his return to sea and was often seen in Peggy's company afterward, hence the rumors of an affair.

Peggy suffered a miscarriage in 1828, during the second straight year of one of her husband's cruises. Obviously, Timberlake was not the father, and tongues began to wag. When her husband died at sea soon afterward of pulmonary disease (rumors said suicide) at age fifty-one, there was an outright buzz over the whole affair.

Peggy cut the mourning period short and married Eaton less than a year later. The two wed so quickly in part as a result of the encouragement of President Jackson, who knew and liked them both. Shortly before his inauguration, Jackson bluntly advised Eaton: "If you love Margaret Timberlake go and marry her at once and shut their [the gossips'] mouths."

If anything, their nuptials had the opposite effect. "She will not be admitted to society!" declared novelist Margaret Bayard Smith. Smith had much company in this among Washington society's *doyennes*, including Floride Calhoun, the stiff-necked, blue-blooded wife of Vice President John C. Calhoun.

Calhoun hoped to use the resulting scandal to his own advantage. With a strong record in the government, Calhoun needed to pave the way for his own presidential run in 1832. He had already succeeded in filling the president's cabinet posts with men who followed his lead. The only problem: the humorless vice president had a rival in the cabinet, someone with vastly better people skills than his own. Secretary of State Van Buren's desire to succeed Jackson was no secret, even if the sly New Yorker never admitted it.

Calhoun hoped to drive a wedge between Jackson and Van Buren and used his prudish wife to do it. Floride snubbed Peggy and convinced the other cabinet wives to do the same. The Calhouns intended to force the Eatons out of Washington. And if Eaton resigned, a Calhoun man could take his place: Van Buren would be all the more isolated.

The plan backfired. While Floride got the wives of all of the other cabinet officials to follow her lead, Van Buren—a widower—had cheerfully embraced the couple. The Calhouns also failed to consider their scheme's impact on the president. Jackson was convinced that campaign slanders had killed his beloved wife Rachel, and seeing Peggy's treatment at the hands of Washington's "polite society" enraged him.

Eaton resigned from the cabinet in 1831, but the Calhouns won a hollow victory. Jackson had formed such a close bond with Van Buren that he was willing to state openly that Van Buren—"frank open, candid, and manly . . . Republican in his principles"—was his preferred successor.

Eaton's political career, once so promising, never recovered from the "Eaton Affair." He governed the Florida Territory and served as Van Buren's ambassador to Spain, dying in 1856.

After Eaton died, Peggy married an Italian musician forty years her junior. Karma eventually caught up with old Mrs. Eaton: her third husband ran off with her seventeen-year-old granddaughter and her fortune. Once a bastard's wife, always a bastard's wife.

> *"I had rather have live vermin on my back than the tongue of one of these Washington women on my reputation."*
>
> —Andrew Jackson to Peggy Eaton

MATTHIAS THE PROPHET
Wholly Fraud
(1778–1841?)

> "If men who keep about their business, maintain their characters, make bargains, make money, and give no other proof of an impaired intellect, can fall into the belief of so revolting, so amazing a fraud and lie, who is safe?"
> —*The North American Review* in an editorial about Matthias the Prophet

Religion has been the basis for some of the greatest of humanity's achievements. Scripture such as the Bible, the Quran, the Tao Te Ching, and the great Hindu epics all contain invocations for people to treat their neighbors well and live good, meaningful lives. But through the millennia, religion has also served as a haven for scoundrels. America as well has a history of supposedly "holy men" making mischief.

Some of them come across as out-and-out whackjobs, others as nothing but malevolent spirits bent on acquiring power. And yet when it comes to sheer bastardry none of the Haggards, Falwells, or Swaggarts could hold a candle to a largely forgotten religious four-flusher who called himself "Matthias the Prophet."

Born Robert Matthews in 1778 on a farm in rural New York, Matthias grew up doing farm work and learning carpentry. At some point he married and fathered children.

But by the mid-1820s Matthews had snapped. Experiencing a "religious vision," he claimed to be the reincarnation of the apostle Matthias, referred to himself as a reborn Jew, and began wandering about the Northeast. He preached a gospel that emphasized the place of the father as the head of any household, the notion of eternal life through passing one's soul along to one's children, and a host of other beliefs based on a loose reading of the King James Bible.

By this time he had quit shaving or cutting his hair, quite a rarity at the time as most men went clean-shaven. This of course made him look every bit the part of the Old Testament prophet.

Matthias eventually made his way to New York City and was able to convince a group of upper-middle-class evangelicals that he was in fact a resurrected apostle. It was only a matter of time before he had bilked them out of thousands of dollars, two houses, and one of the men's wives! For a time Matthias had it all: money he hadn't earned, women drunk on his power, and followers from all walks of life who showed up just to hear him speak. It couldn't last.

By 1835 one of the men whom Matthias cheated had gone bankrupt and had Matthias thrown in jail for fraud. Later that year Matthias and his housekeeper Isabella Van Wagener wound up in more hot water. They were tried for the murder of one of Matthias's wealthiest followers, Elijah Pierson, and for stealing his estate. Matthias was eventually acquitted, but had become a *persona non grata* after being thrown in jail yet again on an unrelated charge of savagely beating his own daughter. Disgraced, he quit New York, and headed west.

BASTARD'S SERVANT

Isabella Van Wagener, Matthias's housekeeper and accomplice in a variety of scams, went on to great fame. She changed her name to Sojourner Truth and established herself as one of the foremost female abolitionists with her "Ain't I a Woman?" speech.

In 1836 Matthias turned up at the Ohio settlement of Joseph Smith's nascent sect of Mormons. Smith welcomed this man who called himself "Jeremiah the Jew" for a few days, even encouraging him to preach a sermon before his own congregation. But the interlude ended with both latter-day prophets denouncing the other as "satanic." Smith went on to be revered as the founder of the Church of Jesus Christ of Latter-Day Saints, while Matthias went on perish in obscure poverty.

In this case the bastard in question spent time in jail, didn't die rich, and didn't escape judgment. Perhaps this was because Matthias's greatest sin was to have been born poor?

"I never shake hands with mere mortals. Know ye 'tis written 'touch not the prophet of the lord'?"

—Robert Matthews (AKA "Matthias the Prophet")

★26★
MARTIN VAN BUREN
The Original Herbert Hoover
(1782–1862)

> "The less government interferes with private pursuits,
> the better for general prosperity."
> —Martin Van Buren

The first American president born after the signing of the Declaration of Independence was also the first career politician to become chief executive. Born into a well-to-do New York family, Van Buren came to be known as the "Fox of Kinderhook" and the "Little Magician" in part because of his ability to make political deals happen.

In other words he was a fixer.

Van Buren was also (as many fixers are) an opportunist of the first order. He rode the populist coattails of Andrew Jackson into the presidency, supporting such scurrilous Jacksonian policies as Indian Removal and the destruction of the nation's fledgling banking system. "Martin Van Ruin" got his comeuppance seven weeks into his administration. On May 10, 1837, the nation faced its first stock market crash.

Picture it if you will: the U.S. government relaxed certain banking regulations. Fewer restrictions allowed for the rise of undercapitalized banks that in turn lent more money than they actually had. Speculation in currency and other areas ran rampant as a result of this loosening of banking rules.

The resulting crash was inevitable: banks that over-lent their resources had trouble collecting some of the money that was owed to them. This resulted in a domino effect that eventually left bank after bank insolvent. Within weeks the entire American financial system was in danger of total collapse.

Sound familiar? It ought to.

But this collapse was not like the stock market crashes of 1929 and 2008. The Panic of 1837 was the first far-reaching, major economic crisis in American history. In 1837 there was no Work Projects administration to employ the destitute masses. No one took drastic measures (rightly or wrongly) to bail out the financial sector in order to avert a total economic catastrophe. President Van Buren refused to involve the government in the private sector's economic woes. It was bad government and would set a terrible precedent, he said. But because he supported and continued Jackson's ridiculous economic policies, Van Buren was partly at fault for allowing it to happen in the first place.

REHABILITATED BASTARD?

Van Buren would later say of his time as president, "the two happiest days of my life were those of my entrance upon the office and my surrender of it." That hardly meant that he stopped having political ambitions, though. He certainly intended to return to the White House. After his retirement from politics in 1841 Van Buren abruptly came to the "shocking" conclusion that slavery was evil(!). He ran as a "Free Soil" candidate for president in 1844 but lost to James K. Polk in the primaries. Of course slavery and the question of it never seemed to bother him much while he was in a position to do something about it.

Jackson hated the Bank of the United States, a federally chartered bank that helped set the value of American currency. In one of the most shortsighted moves in American history, Jackson shut the bank down. He moved the contents of the treasury's balance books to a number of what he called "pet banks." These state and privately chartered banks were allowed to make loans with the federal specie they received. In addition, Jackson loosened federal regulations on who could lend money and who couldn't, making it possible for anyone with a can of paint, a brush, and a board plank big enough to hang out a sign and go into business as a "bank."

The result should have been predictable, especially for a sharp political customer like Van Buren. By mid-1837, the economy was so badly crippled and trade so nearly completely cut off that in many places people gave up the use of currency altogether and reverted to a barter system. It took well into the 1840s for the economy to begin to recover.

★27★
SWARTWOUT-HOYT
Gesundheit!
(1783–1856)

> "The action was assumpsit, to recover from the defendant the sum of thirty-one hundred dollars and seventy-eight cents, received by him for duties, as collector of the port of New York, on an importation of worsted shawls with cotton borders, and worsted suspenders with cotton straps or ends."
>
> —U.S. Court Case *Nelson Elliot V. Samuel Swartwout*, 1836

Imagine a political office so naturally corrupt that crook after crook used it to cash in illegally. Take the Collectorship of the Port of New York, for example. Samuel Swartwout and Jesse Hoyt certainly did.

Swartwout was a Democratic political fixer with a power base in New York and a history of dabbling in political intrigue. One of Aaron Burr's lieutenants in his failed "Western Conspiracy," Swartwout served as a runner between Burr and James Wilkinson in their talks for putting Burr's plot into action. Wilkinson eventually arrested Swartwout and held him without trial on a U.S. warship for his trouble. Eventually cleared, Swartwout even shared Burr's European exile for a while.

By the time Andrew Jackson ran for the presidency in 1828 he needed fixers like Swartwout. Swartwout helped get out the New York vote, and Jackson rewarded him with the plum political post of customs collector for the Port of New York.

Swartwout embezzled just over $2 million (worth close to ten times that in today's currency) during his eight years in office. But Swartwout was really only the tip of the bastardberg. Corrupt officials riddled the Customs Office; everyone seemed to be shaving a bit off the top of duties owed to the U.S. government.

When Swartwout's political enemy Martin Van Buren succeeded Jackson as president in 1837, he did not renew Swartwout's appointment. Van Buren was also a New Yorker and had heard the rumors about corruption in the state Customs Office. Swartwout immediately sailed for England, ostensibly to inspect some property he owned there. But he forgot to close out his Customs Office expense account before he did so, and investigators found evidence of impropriety while he was gone.

Swartwout stayed in England, no doubt buoyed by the $2 million he'd actually taken with him. When the story broke in the papers, Swartwout became known as the "Prince of Thieves." But that's only part of the story.

Jesse Hoyt, a New York lawyer and Van Buren's political ally, was appointed in order to oversee cleanup of the whole business, but he didn't bother to sack everyone working in the office and start over. (Sound familiar? Think about it: how many people at Goldman Sachs lost their jobs after the bailout last year?) So when Hoyt's term came to an end in 1841, a Congressional committee appointed by President John Tyler scrutinized Hoyt and his employees for "financial improprieties." They quickly found that Hoyt's (and Swartwout's before him) head cashier, a fellow named Ogden, had been skimming for the better part of a decade.

In one of history's rich (read "sickening") political ironies, Congress was miffed that Tyler had neglected to get their approval for the committee investigating graft in Hoyt's office. More pissed off than logical, Congressional leaders tabled any resolutions intended to come out of the committee's findings, keeping Hoyt from being punished. Upon hearing this, Swartwout managed to convince federal prosecutors that the money he had supposedly stolen was actually taken by Ogden. Swartwout forfeited some of his New York property (for tax purposes) in exchange for a guarantee that he would not be prosecuted for any wrongdoing; he returned to New York later that same year. Swartwout died in New York City in 1856, never having spent a day in jail or paid back any of the money he actually stole. As for Hoyt, aside from being removed from office by Van Buren before the end of his term, he suffered no further reprimand, was not even charged with a crime, and died wealthy in New York City in 1885.

Bastards.

★ 28 ★

RICHARD JOHNSON
The U.S. Vice President Married to His Own Slave
(1780–1850)

"Johnson's dead weight."
—Andrew Jackson

In 1836 presidential candidate Martin Van Buren of New York needed a military hero to help balance the party ticket in the national elections. Richard Johnson was just the man for the job. The celebrated veteran of the War of 1812 had represented Kentucky in both the House and the Senate and was rumored to have killed the great Shawnee Indian chief Tecumseh at the Battle of the Thames in 1813.

He also kept a slave as his common-law wife.

Johnson even brought his own ready-made slogan with him to the Van Buren campaign: "Rumsey Dumsey, Rumsey Dumsey, Colonel Johnson killed Tecumseh." Outgoing President Andrew Jackson supported Van Buren's pick mostly because Johnson wasn't William C. Rives, Van Buren's preferred choice for a running mate whom Jackson loathed.

But Johnson had his own baggage. He openly carried on a relationship with a slave woman named Julia Chinn, whom he had inherited from his father. Chinn was an *octoroon* (a person with one grandparent who had been black) and could easily pass for white, but she remained Johnson's property until her death during a cholera outbreak in 1833. In all respects (save granting her freedom) Johnson treated Chinn as his common-law wife, and they had two daughters together.

While Johnson's constituents didn't seem to mind his relationship with Chinn at first, his Senate career lasted only a single term largely as a result of it. And when he was elected vice president by the Senate in 1836, it was by an incredibly narrow, partisan margin. When prodded about Chinn, Johnson alluded to other politicians' alleged (or in Jefferson's case, recently proven) relationships with one or more of their slaves: "Unlike Jefferson, Clay, Poindexter and others, I married my wife under the eyes of God, and apparently He has found no objections."

Such high-sounding words notwithstanding, Johnson never stopped being and thinking like a Kentucky slave-owner.

After Chinn died Johnson took up with another of his slaves. When that woman left him because she had fallen in love with another man, Johnson had her tracked down and returned to him. After he sold the woman at auction, he pursued a relationship with her sister!

Now *that* is a bastard.

PROPERTY-OWNING BASTARD

When Johnson and Julia's two daughters grew up and married (both to white men), he gave each of them land as a wedding present. However, the public record states that when he died in 1850 "he left no widow, children, father, or mother living." One of his daughters, Adeline, had predeceased him in 1836, the same year he was elected vice president. But his daughter Imogene was alive and well in 1850. And yet Johnson's two brothers inherited his property after his death.

After his election as vice president Johnson's mental and physical health began to suffer, and he became the laughing stock of the nation's capitol. In time he became such a liability that Van Buren passed him over when choosing his running mate in 1840.

Johnson was in and out of the Kentucky State House for the next decade, returning to office one last time in November 1850. By this time he was literally a dead man walking. Johnson's state attracted the notice of the *Louisville Daily Journal*:

"Col. R. M. Johnson is laboring under an attack of dementia, which renders him totally unfit for business. It is painful to see him on the floor attempting to discharge the duties of a member. He is incapable of properly exercising his physical or mental powers."

He died two weeks later.

★ 29 ★
JOHN TYLER
Dirty Old President
(1790–1862)

> "Miss Gardiner, who you recollect was said was going to marry the President, has kicked the old man. Had Gardiner lived, it is believed by many here in the capital that he would have made his daughter marry old Tyler to get the Collectorship at New York for himself."
> —Senator Spencer Jarnagin

In 1843 the recently widowed president of the United States fell in love. John Tyler had lost his first wife, the mother of his first seven children, to the results of a paralytic stroke in September of 1842.

Within a year Tyler had lost his heart all over again, this time to a woman thirty years his junior!

The new object of the president's affection was a Long Island beauty named Julia Gardiner. Often called "the Belle of Long Island," Julia was the youngest child of New York millionaire David Gardiner. Julia was pretty, smart, vivacious in ways that only the youngest daughter of indulgent parents can be; in other words, she was spoiled rotten.

Dazzled by the fact that she was being wooed by the most powerful man in the country, Julia returned Tyler's affections, in spite of their age difference. Her parents brought her to Washington on a number of occasions in order to get her "out" in Washington society, where she charmed men and women alike everywhere she went. It was only a matter of time before she began to have gentlemen callers, and one of them was the completely besotted president.

While an age difference this wide between would-be mates was certainly nothing new to human history in 1843, it certainly was new to the office of the president. Only one widower (Martin Van Buren) before Tyler had served as president, and that president had not chased after a woman nearly young enough to be his grand-child. As a result, there was considerable talk among the capital city's smart set.

The major obstacle to this May–December romance was Julia's father, David Gardiner. Tired of just being rich, Gardiner had begun to dabble in politics, serving a term in the New York State Senate. Now he had set his sights on a position in the Federal government, and he wasn't above using his daughter to get it.

The rumors flew fast and furious in the ensuing months: Gardiner wanted to be Comptroller for the Port of New York; he wanted a cabinet post; he wanted to be a United States Senator. The sky was apparently the limit. Whatever his asking price, it was obvious that Gardiner expected Tyler to help him get it, and in exchange for his daughter's hand in marriage.

For public consumption Gardiner adopted the posture that his daughter was too young for the fifty-three-year-old president. He arranged a series of social engagements for her with "safe" escorts such as closeted gay Senator James Buchanan of Pennsylvania.

It's anyone's guess how this would have all played out had Gardiner not died in an explosion onboard a U.S. Navy ship in February 1844. The obstacle so abruptly removed, Tyler made himself available to console the distraught Julia. Within a month the two were engaged, and they eloped in May of that year.

BASTARD GETTIN' BUSY

Tyler was married to Julia for the remaining eighteen years of his life. When he died at the age of seventy-two in 1862, Julia had recently given birth to their seventh child, which gave Tyler fourteen children that survived infancy—a White House record!

So who was the bastard of this piece: Tyler for coveting this beautiful young girl? Or Gardiner, for his willingness to use Julia, his own flesh and blood, for his own ends? You decide.

★ 30 ★
ABEL P. UPSHUR
Texas Redbacks and Currency Manipulation
(1790–1844)

> "The terms of the treaty (of annexation) call for the United States to pay all the debts of Texas. Texas bonds and treasury notes that had been below 10 cents will be par. Now Sir, was there ever such a chance for a magnificent speculation?"
> —Abel P. Upshur

Currency speculation in one form or another is as old as the notion of currency itself. By the mid-nineteenth century investing in the future value of foreign money was a fairly lucrative activity in every major city in the world. This was especially true of Washington, D.C. An unofficial currency exchange took place day in, day out, on the northern end of Lafayette Square, within sight of the White House.

While speculating is perfectly legal, *manipulating* the value of currency is not. And that brings us to a guy you've never heard of named Abel P. Upshur. This former Virginia judge, congressman, and secretary of the navy exploited the system while working as John Tyler's secretary of state from 1843–1844.

In 1836, American settlers in the Mexican state of Coahuila y Tejas rebelled and won their independence from Mexico. Texas immediately petitioned to join the Union as a slave-holding state. But by 1836 the slavery debate was heating up. So Texas remained a separate nation. And since sovereign nations require money in order to operate, the Texas government invented a currency note called the "redback."

Texas, however, lacked the gold to back its own currency at anything close to full value. The Texans tried to counter the resulting inflation by simply printing more redbacks, but this just decreased the redback's relative value as a means of trade. By the early 1840s a Texas redback was worth eight cents to an American bank.

For the forward-thinking investor, though, redbacks were anything but worthless. After all, if the United States annexed Texas and made it a new state, Texas's currency system would be discontinued. The Texans would need to adopt the United States's monetary system, and the U.S. Treasury would have to retire all those redbacks at face value. A Texas redback purchased from someone changing them in the north end of Lafayette Square in 1843 would be worth $1 in American coin and currency to a U.S.-Treasury-backed bank after annexation. The potential profit was *twenty times* the purchase price.

BASTARD BY ASSOCIATION

Upshur's friend and replacement as navy secretary was former Virginia Congressman Thomas Gilmer. He also speculated deeply in Texas redbacks, likely on Upshur's advice. Like Upshur, Gilmer failed to profit from speculating in redbacks. He died in the same gunnery accident that killed Upshur on the day the treaty was signed.

Now imagine that you're the U.S. Secretary of State, secretly negotiating with the Texans to hammer out a treaty. You could use that information to turn a healthy profit by quietly and gradually speculating in Texas redbacks.

Upshur got halfway there. On the morning of February 28, 1844, he and Texan ambassador to the United States Isaac Van Zandt secretly signed a treaty of annexation. If Congress ratified the treaty, his redbacks were going to be worth a fortune.

The U.S. Senate, however, had other ideas. In April 1844, the Senate voted Upshur's treaty down. For the moment at least, Upshur's supply of redbacks was worth less than the paper on which they were printed.

By that point Upshur was beyond caring about Texas, redbacks, currency speculation, or anything else, for that matter. He was killed (along with the secretary of the navy and several other VIPs) by a freak explosion during the test-firing of a new naval cannon on the afternoon of February 28, 1844. It was the very day on which he signed the treaty of annexation.

★ 31 ★
JAMES BUCHANAN
America's First Gay President
(1791–1868)

> "I am selfish enough to hope you will not be able to procure an associate who will cause you to feel no regret at our separation. For myself, I shall feel lonely in the midst of Paris, for there I shall have no Friend with whom I can commune as with my own thoughts."
>
> —Rufus deVayne King while serving as minister to France,
> to James Buchanan

Our fifteenth president, James Buchanan of Pennsylvania, was one of the most experienced and capable of nineteenth century diplomats. He was also a disaster as a president: his paralysis in the face of mounting Southern pressure to protect slavery helped lead to the Civil War, which began during his term. In a more social context, he was the only bachelor to ever occupy the White House and our first gay president.

William Rufus deVayne King was Buchanan's longtime friend. The scion of a well-to-do North Carolinian family who won election to Congress while still in his twenties, King eventually moved to Alabama, where he helped found the city of Selma. King served as a U.S. Senator for decades before retiring and taking the post of minister to France. He was elected as Franklin Pierce's vice president in 1852. He was also our first gay vice president.

Buchanan met King in the 1820s while the two served together in Congress. From that moment on they were inseparable and eventually began sharing a house. The time they spent living together raised no eyebrows. But their behavior together and apart certainly did.

No matter how discreet the two might have thought they were, their relationship was an open secret, and the cause of much coarse humor around the nation's capital.

President Jackson often referred to King as "Aunt Fancy"; a Buchanan biographer more politely noted that King was "fastidious about his appearance." And Tennessee Congressman Aaron Brown even called Buchanan "Miss Nancy," which was the nineteenth century's slang equivalent of calling someone a "fag" today. In one famous letter, Brown wrote about observing "Senator and Mrs. Buchanan" (e.g., King) in the midst of a quarrel that closely resembled a lover's spat.

BASTARD "DATING"

Though Buchanan and King are remembered as lifelong bachelors, Buchanan had been engaged until his wealthy fiancée abruptly committed suicide. According to many who knew the couple, Buchanan was far more interested in the girl's money than in her. We'll never know for sure why she killed herself, as Buchanan made a point of burning all of their letters to each other. He called on many young ladies in fashionable Washington society after her death, but Buchanan never seriously courted any woman again. When asked about it, he said that he had never gotten over his dead fiancée. Some noted that it was almost as if he was using the event as a shield, keeping him from having to go through the pretense of dating.

As much as their bond shocked polite society, the two remained devoted to each other for the rest of King's life. In 1852, when Buchanan lost out to Senator Franklin Pierce for the Democratic presidential nomination, he was mollified by the selection of King as Pierce's running mate. They won the election, but King was ill with tuberculosis. A special act of Congress allowed King to be sworn in as vice president in Cuba, where his doctors had advised he go for his health; he was the only American vice president to take the oath of office outside of the country. It was too late: King died just over a month after taking office. He never returned to the United States.

How Buchanan reacted to this tragic news is, of course, unrecorded. And in retrospect the very pretense so central to the lives of both of these men, the need to keep up appearances (as much as possible in a gossipy town like Washington, D.C.) just seems sad.

★32★
WILLIAM WALKER
When "Filibuster" Was More than Just a Word
(1824–1860)

"What Walker saw and heard at Guaymas satisfied him that a comparatively small body of Americans might gain a position on the Sonora frontier, and protect the families on the border from the Indians; and such an act would be one of humanity, no less than of justice, whether sanctioned or not by the Mexican Government."

—William Walker

Born in Nashville in 1824, William Walker trained in Philadelphia as a doctor, but seems never to have practiced medicine. Instead he traveled throughout Europe during the next two years, then moved to New Orleans to study law. In 1849, he caught gold fever and moved to San Francisco along with thousands of others. It was there that he conceived and carried out his first attempt at a "filibustering" expedition.

In 1853 Walker and a small force of men took the city of La Paz, declaring it the capital of the new "Republic of Lower California." But when he ran out of money, supplies, and ammunition, Walker abandoned this "republic" and fled back to California one step ahead of the Mexican army. Walker next set his sights on tiny Nicaragua in Central America. In 1855 he led a well-financed, well-armed force of over three hundred men (most of them Americans) into the war-torn country.

Within a year Walker had himself "elected" president. Having seized power, his methods for holding on to it were effective and brutal. At one point he ordered one of his officers, the English-born adventurer Charles Frederick Henningsen, to sack and burn the city of Granada. Henningsen torched the place, killed many of the residents, ran off the rest, and then decamped, hotly pursued by several thousand Honduran soldiers. He supposedly left behind a sign marking the smoking ruin of the city that read "*Aquí fue Granada*" ("Here was Granada").

By 1857 Walker had worn out his welcome. Not only had he made local enemies, he had also irritated American millionaire "Commodore" Cornelius Vanderbilt. Vanderbilt had made his fortune in shipping. In Nicaragua his company used short rail lines and lake steamers to transport people and goods from the Gulf of Mexico, across immense Lake Nicaragua, thence to Pacific steamboats, which were ready to take travelers the rest of the way to California.

WHAT'S IN A WORD?

The word "filibuster" itself comes from the Anglicization of a French word *filibustier*, which means "freebooter" or "pirate." In truth this notion of privately funded and manned expeditions of conquest into America's neighboring countries began before Walker was even born. "Adventurers" had coveted both frontier and Mexican land for years. Men like former Vice President Aaron Burr worked tirelessly on cockamamie plans to either carve a new country out of the western territories of the United States or carve a slice out of northern Mexico . . . or both.

When Walker nationalized Vanderbilt's lake steamers, the "Commodore" set his agents to oust Walker and get Vanderbilt's property back. Realizing it was time to get while the getting was good, Walker surrendered to the captain of an American warship, returned to a hero's welcome in New York, and wrote a book about his exploits. Within a year he had begun hatching another scheme to return to power in Nicaragua.

This time Walker's famous sense of timing failed him. He landed in Honduras in 1860, and instantly found himself in the custody of the British navy. Rather than return Walker to the United States, the British—who controlled Honduras's neighbor British Honduras, now Belize—turned Walker over to the Honduran government as a gesture of good will. A firing squad executed the last filibuster on the site of what is now a hospital in the port city of Trujillo, on September 12, 1860. Walker was just thirty-six years old; he missed the American Civil War by a mere three months.

★33★
DAN SICKLES
The Temporary Insanity Defense
(1819–1914)

> "One might as well try to spoil a rotten egg as to damage
> Dan's character."
> —George Templeton Strong

Democratic Congressman Dan Sickles was already a nationally notorious figure when he pulled strings to get appointed as a brigadier general of volunteers at the beginning of the Civil War. In 1859 Dan Sickles became the first person in American history to successfully employ the "temporary insanity" defense in order to beat a murder charge.

The son of a New York City attorney who dabbled in local politics, Sickles followed in his father's footsteps, securing a scholarship to study law at New York University. While a student there he first met his future wife Teresa when he rented a room from her family. She was three years old. He was twenty.

The two of them eloped thirteen years later; Teresa was sixteen and pregnant.

By the late 1850s Sickles had been elected to Congress, and the couple had relocated to Washington, D.C., moving into a house on Lafayette Square, less than a block from the White House. Isolated from her family and by then aware that Sickles drank too much and chased women habitually, it comes as no surprise that Teresa eventually began an affair of her own.

Teresa's lover wasn't just anyone; he was Philip Barton Key, son of the author of "The Star-Spangled Banner." Key was also district attorney for the District of Columbia, and every bit as much a womanizer as Teresa's husband.

When Sickles found out about his wife's infidelity his reaction was typically Victorian: he flew into a rage and insisted his wife write out a detailed confession. She did so. It wasn't enough.

In February 1859, Sickles confronted his wife's lover on a street corner down the block from his house; right across Pennsylvania Avenue from the White House. Sickles shot Key twice, once in the groin. Key died the next day.

On trial for murder, Sickles hired an expensive legal defense team, including future Secretary of War Edwin M. Stanton. Their strategy was for Sickles to claim that learning of his wife's infidelity had so enraged him that he could not control his own thoughts, that he was literally "temporarily insane."

BASTARD BODY PARTS

History best remembers Sickles for what he did as a "political general" during the Battle of Gettysburg. He disobeyed a direct order and led the men under his command to a position far forward of where they had been assigned to defend the flank of the Union lines. Sickles lost his leg to a cannon ball while in the Peach Orchard. He later donated his severed limb to the National Museum of Health and Medicine, where he frequently came to visit it for the remaining fifty years of his life.

Sickles began his trial as the butt of much public scorn, but his defense was so sensational and so successful that he was acquitted on all charges. He was even seen as something of a hero, having rid the innocent women of Washington of a predatory rascal like Key.

Teresa Sickles never reconciled with her husband. She died profoundly sad and lonely in 1867. Sickles for his part went on to lead a long political career in spite of losing his leg. He served as U.S. Minister to Spain from 1869 to 1874. In 1871 he married the daughter of a Spanish nobleman who eventually bore him three children.

Sickles received the Congressional Medal of Honor for losing his leg at Gettysburg, and money was appropriated to erect a statue in his honor on the spot in the Peach Orchard where he was wounded. But the statue was never cast or placed.

Rumor has it that Sickles stole the money.

DAVID C. BRODERICK
The Only Senator Killed in a Duel
(1820–1859)

"To sit in the Senate of the United States as a Senator for one day, I
would consent to be roasted in a slow fire on the plaza."
—David C. Broderick

Over the course of its two-hundred-plus years of history, the United States has been
served by hundreds of senators. A few score of them have died in office. But only one
serving U.S. Senator was ever killed in a duel: that bastard out of California, David
C. Broderick.

The son of an immigrant Irish stonecutter who came to America in order to work
on the U.S. Capitol building, Broderick was born in Washington, D.C., and raised
in New York City. While still a young man, he became the proprietor of a public
house where customers discussed politics over beer and made political deals in the
back room.

Broderick headed west in 1849, and once he landed in California began a highly
lucrative business casting gold and silver coins. He had a talent for making his coins
just a bit light, so that a $10 gold piece would be full of about $8 worth of actual
gold, and so on. Within a year he was a millionaire. He employed both his new-
found wealth and the political acumen he had learned from his time running that
pub in New York to get himself elected to the California State Senate as a Democrat.
Within another year he was serving as that body's president.

And he had already established himself as the uncrowned king of San Francisco.

Broderick ruled the city with an iron fist, receiving kickbacks from every office-
holder in need of his political muscle to get elected. He could be vindictive, even
cruel, and he had a terrible temper.

By the mid-1850s the California Democratic Party faced a huge rift between Southern Democrats (many of whom wanted to see slavery introduced into the state) and the Free Soil Democrats. In 1857 Broderick's unchallenged leadership of the Free Soilers led to his election to the U.S. Senate, fulfilling one of his lifelong dreams. He was only thirty-six years old.

For two years Broderick served in the Senate. He returned home in 1859 during the Congressional late summer recess and helped defeat his former friend David Terry's bid for reelection as chief justice of the State Supreme Court. They were after all political opponents: Terry was a Southerner and a pro-slavery Democrat.

STUPID BASTARD

One month shy of the thirtieth anniversary of his killing of Broderick, Terry assaulted an associate justice of the U.S. Supreme Court. This justice, a former friend (as Broderick had been) of Terry's named Stephen J. Field had not only just ruled against Terry and his wife in a suit they had filed against her supposed first husband, a silver millionaire, but had jailed the two for contempt of court. So when Terry encountered Field and his U.S. Marshal bodyguard on a train trestle in Lathrop, California, on August 14, 1889, he lost his famously bad temper. Terry advanced on Field and before anyone could intervene, slapped him hard across the face. The marshal shot him, and he died on the spot.

At the state convention in Sacramento later that year Terry made some cutting remarks regarding Broderick's character. Broderick was livid when he read Terry's speech in a newspaper, and sent off an incendiary note in reply. In no time Terry had challenged Broderick to a duel and the latter had accepted.

These two political titans fought at Lake Merced, outside of San Francisco's city limits on September 13, 1859. Broderick's pistol discharged prematurely. Terry's shot pierced Broderick's lung. Broderick lingered for three days before dying on September 16, 1859, not forty years old.

★35★
SIMON CAMERON
Secretary of War Profiteering
(1799–1889)

> "An honest politician is one who when he is
> bought stays bought."
>
> —Simon Cameron

There are all kinds of bastards, but some just rise above (or, if you prefer, "sink below") most of the others. These include, but are in no way limited to, rapists, murderers, and slave traffickers. Right there in the pit with them are people who profit by stealing from the soldiers protecting their country. People like Simon Cameron, President Lincoln's first secretary of war.

Born poor in Pennsylvania in 1799, Cameron charmed his way into a series of lucrative political posts. He then helped found the Northern Central Railway, sold it, and started a bank. Cameron was a wealthy man by the time he turned to politics full-time in his forties. By the election year of 1860 Cameron had been a Whig, a "Know-Nothing," a Democrat, and of course, a Republican. He had also served two separate terms in the U.S. Senate and wanted to be president.

At the Republican National Convention in Chicago Cameron didn't have the votes to get the nomination, so he parlayed his control of a substantial number of Pennsylvania votes into a place in the cabinet of the eventual nominee, Abraham Lincoln of Illinois. In return for his support Cameron was only too happy to take over the War Department. He had barely taken his oath of office when the Civil War broke out.

Cameron served as secretary of war for a little less than a year. During those ten months Northern newspaper after Northern newspaper reported widespread graft involving contracts given for both goods and services intended to support the Union war effort. Over-aged muskets were purchased that didn't fire. Blankets were purchased, paid for, and never received. Uniforms were threadbare. Horses were sold to the government, only to be found to be blind or lame, or some combination thereof. Barrels of salt pork were purchased and when opened, found to be empty, filled with salt water, half-full, or outright spoiled. And on top of all of this, the War Department was spending millions.

How did Cameron avoid seeming as if he were personally profiting from this national disgrace?

Railroads. Everything the government bought and shipped to the troops in the field went via rail.

And if it ran through Pennsylvania, because of his railroad contracts, Simon Cameron got a piece of it. Merchants and traders Cameron rewarded with such lucrative contracts all overpaid for shipping on railroads in which he'd invested, creating Cameron's "cut."

By December 1862, Lincoln had seen enough. He unceremoniously told Cameron that he had decided to honor Cameron's previously expressed "desire for a change of position," and was nominating him to serve as the new ambassador to Russia. Cameron had expressed no such desire. Regardless, he was out within a month.

Cameron was eventually censured by the House of Representatives for his part in the scandal. It could have been worse. After the House Committee on Contracts made public the number of unfit horses and faulty weapons that were sold to the War Department on Cameron's watch, the House itself passed a bill making it tantamount to treason to pull these sorts of swindles.

Cameron didn't stay in Russia for long. He was back in the United States within a year, and by 1866 was once again in the Senate, serving a third term. He held on to his office until he had received assurances that his son Donald would succeed him. J. Donald Cameron served in the Senate for twenty years.

Simon Cameron himself lived to be ninety years old. He died of natural causes, rich and by any measure, successful. And he never spent a day in jail for his part in profiteering from the republic's darkest hour.

Bastard.

★36★
ULYSSES S. GRANT
Drunk on Duty
(1822–1885)

> "The vice of intemperance had not a little to do with
> my decision to resign."
> —Ulysses S. Grant

Ulysses S. Grant: master strategist who turned the tide of the American Civil War by re-writing the book on military strategy and tactics; two-term Republican president of the United States (more on *that* later!); bestselling author whose Civil War memoir stands up to comparisons to the work of such heavy-hitters in the field as Julius Caesar and Tacitus.

Drunk.

That's right: the man who would one day partner with President Abraham Lincoln to help preserve the Union was once drummed out of the same army he would later command as General-in-Chief for drunkenness. Not officially, of course. Officially he resigned his commission.

As a young man, Grant had attended the U.S. Military Academy at West Point at the behest of his successful businessman father, who worried that Grant had no ambition and felt that the security of a military career might be good for his "unfocused" son.

Stationed in Missouri, Grant quickly met the love of his life, Julia Dent. He courted her ardently for years. The entire time he was away fighting in the Mexican War in the mid-1840s the young lovers exchanged frequent letters.

During this time, Grant developed a reputation for having an affinity for the bottle. His appreciation for alcohol was unremarkable for the time: most soldiers in the mid-nineteenth century drank as often as they could get their hands on a supply of liquor. It's a truism that is nearly a cliché. Aside from notations about the generally unkempt manner of his uniform (one of his biographers has likened Grant's "military bearing" to that of a sack of potatoes, and in the spit-and-polish regular army, that could be the kiss of death for an officer's career), Grant's record was spotless during the Mexican War.

BASTARD-IN-LAW

We know for a fact that while Grant himself was personally honest, he was also a relatively guileless individual; he entrusted people of poor character with responsibilities they had no right to possess. This included his brother-in-law, a New York "businessman" named Abel Corbin who married Grant's sister Virginia. Not only did Corbin steal Grant blind by "investing" his money, he also introduced Grant to a succession of swindlers bent on getting in on the action; some tagged along all the way to cabinet posts in his administration.

After the war Grant went back to Missouri and at long last married his beloved Julia. By 1854 he had been promoted to captain (one of about fifty left in the army after the Mexican War). His new rank took him to Ft. Humboldt in California, and forced Grant to leave a very pregnant Julia behind in Missouri. His officer's salary was so low that they could not afford for her to join her husband on the West Coast. It was here that Grant—pining for his wife, worried about her health, and serving as the fort's paymaster—ran into trouble as a result of his drinking.

Grant's commanding officer in California was a by-the-book career solider named Robert C. Buchanan. One evening Buchanan found Grant drunk on duty and offered him the chance to resign in lieu of being kicked out for his offense. Grant quit and remained in good standing, officially. In many ways it was probably a relief to him, as he never cared for garrison life anyway. He returned home to Julia and their children, and he set about being a failure at every single professional venture to which he turned his hand.

But history was not finished with Grant. Opportunity knocked with the outbreak of the Civil War in 1861. Within a month of volunteering Grant was a general.

★37★
WILLIAM MARCY TWEED
Honest Graft and Dishonest Graft
(1823–1878)

> "Everybody is talkin' these days about Tammany men growin' rich on graft, but nobody thinks of drawin' the distinction between honest graft and dishonest graft. There's all the difference in the world between the two."
> —George Washington Plunkitt, Tammany Hall machine politician, quoted in *Plunkitt of Tammany Hall*

William Macy Tweed was not just any native New Yorker. He began his rise to power simply enough, serving as a volunteer fireman in 1848. But by the end of the Civil War, barely two decades later, this singular bastard and his henchmen (later known as the so-called "Tweed Ring") virtually ran New York City through the Tammany Hall political machine.

George Washington Plunkitt was the very prototype of the "ward heeler," someone right out of a Damon Runyon short story, and was involved in big city machine politics. The colorful quotes from *Plunkitt of Tammany Hall* preserve his world perfectly:

"Yes, many of our men have grown rich in politics. I have myself. I've made a big fortune out of the game, and I'm gettin' richer every day, but I've not gone in for dishonest graft—blackmailin' gamblers, saloonkeepers, disorderly people, etc.—and neither has any of the men who have made big fortunes in politics.

There's an honest graft, and I'm an example of how it works. I might sum up the whole thing by sayin': 'I seen my opportunities and I took 'em.' Just let me explain by examples. My party's in power in the city, and it's goin' to undertake a lot of public improvements. Well, I'm tipped off, say, that they're going to lay out a new park at a certain place. I see my opportunity and I take it. I go to that place and I buy up all the land I can in the neighborhood. Then the board of this or that makes its plan public, and there is a rush to get my land, which nobody cared particular for before."

The ability of ward politicians—such as the men who ran the Democratic Party's Tammany Hall political machine in New York City—to give immediate attention to the problems of the poor in an era where social workers were unknown is arguable, but that sort of "attention" always came at a steep price. The dark underside of Tammany politics—the side that Plunkitt blithely dismissed as "dishonest graft"—still existed. And that less romantic style of political wheeling and dealing had an exemplar in Tweed, the man at the top of the Tammany power structure during much of its nineteenth century heyday.

Tweed knew how to work the urban poor: he gave them money, employed their relatives, and bought them drinks. He never had a problem purchasing their votes, and by 1870 it seemed his power was unassailable. Tweed skimmed a healthy bit of taxpayers' money off the top of city revenues (to the tune of approximately $30 million per year). He even managed to get himself named to the board of directors for the Erie Railroad (by doing political favors for such fellow bastards as financiers Jay Gould and "Diamond Jim" Fisk).

Tweed began to run into trouble when the *New York Times* ran a huge exposé on his activities in and outside of Tammany Hall. The political cartoons by muckraking journalist Thomas Nast, who made his reputation in part at the expense of Tweed's public image, especially galled the "Boss."

Tweed was tried on graft charges on two separate occasions, the second time fleeing to Cuba, only to be extradited and returned to serve his sentence. He died in prison in 1878, having served only two years of a six-year-long sentence.

A fitting end for a greedy bastard of his caliber.

"As long as I count the votes what are you going to do about it?"

—William Marcy Tweed

★38★
JAY GOULD
The Bastard Who Caused "Black Friday"
(1836–1892)

"I can hire one half of the working class to kill the other half."
—Jay Gould

Jay Gould was a financier who rose from humble origins to command a vast fortune. Personally honest, a loving husband, and father devoted to his family, Gould was also a first-rate bastard whose efforts to corner the gold market helped trigger a devastating economic depression.

During the Civil War, the US government had issued paper money backed by no specie, just the government's assurances. Many people speculated in greenbacks, believing that the government would eventually pay the full face value in gold "double eagle" coins for these bank notes. And as always, some of the speculation was far less than legal.

Gould and his business partner "Diamond Jim" Fisk hatched a scheme that would allow them to use this situation to corner the gold market. In order to carry this out, the two men needed someone working within the Treasury Department to tip them off about imminent buy-backs. Gould and Fisk pulled political strings to get President Ulysses S. Grant's fellow Civil War general Dan Butterfield into the plot and got him appointed assistant treasurer of the United States. In that position Butterfield would have knowledge of when the government planned a large buy-back of greenbacks and could tip off Gould and Fisk so they could drive up the price right beforehand, thereby maximizing their profit potential.

The scheme also required access to Grant in social situations. That was where his brother-in-law Abel Corbin came in. Corbin provided that access at numerous dinner parties throughout much of early 1869. During these informal meetings, Gould and Fisk would urge the president to buy back all of the outstanding greenbacks, saying that it would make for a more sound post-war economy.

At first, Grant agreed and ordered government buy-backs to begin. But by the late summer of 1869 he began to grow suspicious of Gould, Fisk, and Butterfield. In September of that year Grant had the government sell $4 million worth of gold on the stock market (thereby causing a glut and driving prices down) without letting Butterfield in on the secret.

The gold market crashed as a result on September 24, 1869, the date known ever afterward as "Black Friday." Gould and Fisk had been buying up gold and hoarding it in the weeks before the government's action, causing the price to rise dramatically. People who had bought gold at Gould and Fisk's engineered and inflated prices scrambled to dump their gold stock, and within minutes the premium paid on gold shares plummeted to a fraction of what it had been just twenty-four hours earlier. This turmoil dragged down the entire market and resulted in a devastating stock market crash.

WHAT ABOUT THAT OTHER BASTARD?

Whereas Gould weathered his legal troubles, his partner Big Jim Fisk didn't live long enough to be sued. In 1871 he got into a dispute with a former business partner who had recently married Fisk's mistress. The man was frustrated that he had been unsuccessful in his attempts to blackmail Fisk. So on January 6, 1872, he tracked Fisk down and shot him in the office where he'd stolen so many people's money and had so many trysts with his killer's future wife.

Gould and Fisk lost relatively little in the crash because they got out early enough to stave off too much of a loss. Corbin was wiped out, as were countless other investors.

But this is not one of those stories wherein the bastards in question get off scot-free. Gould—who had already been pilloried in the press for his association with Boss Tweed of Tammany Hall—paid out millions in the lawsuits that resulted from the failure. He went on to die much poorer, merely the ninth richest man in America. Black Friday cost him, dearly.

★39★
OAKES AMES
The "King of Spades" and the Crédit Mobilier of America Scandal
(1804–1873)

"The road must be built, and you are the man to do it. Take hold of it yourself. By building the Union Pacific, you will be the remembered man of your generation."
—President Abraham Lincoln to Oakes Ames, 1865

Imagine that the government sets up a corporation to produce something important and risky to build. In order to make the project attractive to investors, the government sweetens the pot with mineral and water rights to already valuable land in return for the completion of this project. Is that how sly businessmen lose their shirts? No. That's how the first American transcontinental railroad got built.

It's easy to picture one of the ass-hats running this "sure thing" company deciding that he was not making enough money in return for the miniscule amount of risk he was taking. The question left to answer: how does the bastard further maximize his profits?

If he's Republican Congressman Oakes Ames of Massachusetts, he breaks the law repeatedly, using his family's company to his own ends. Ames incorporated shell companies, hired these "outside contractors" (who were really Ames and his cronies) to do some of the construction, and overpaid these middlemen by ten times the going rate for materials and labor. In the end, he left the stockholders of the original company in the hole and on the hook for his failings; he and his "contractors," on the other hand, were rich.

Since so many wheels needed to move at the same time, Ames used a predictable means to grease the cogs: money. He funneled contracts to Crédit Mobilier of America, a construction company that in turn purchased stock in the Union Pacific Railroad. He overspent on everything, and used the ongoing cycle of money to enrich those important to the project (along with most of their relatives).

Too much got spent too injudiciously for Ames's profligacy to go unnoted for long. By 1867 government officials were suspicious about the ridiculous amounts of money Crédit Mobilier was charging the Union Pacific for "essential services."

WHAT'S IN A NICKNAME?

Ames was the son of a Massachusetts blacksmith who made a killing producing and selling shovels. Ames went into his father's business as a partner, took over for the old man, and made even more money selling shovels. By the time he entered Congress in 1863 Ames had picked up the nickname "King of Spades" as a result of his success. By the time of his death ten years later, he would be known by another nickname: "Hoax Ames." Ames had his own brother made the Union Pacific Railroad's first president, and took on the transcontinental project at the request of President Lincoln himself in early 1865. And Ames had a reputation for getting things done.

With the project's success hanging in the balance, Ames acted swiftly and decisively: he bribed several influential congressmen (including future President James A. Garfield) with sweetheart deals on Crédit Mobilier stock. This forestalled a formal Congressional inquiry for years afterward, and allowed Ames and his crowd to finish the railroad in 1869. In 1872 the *New York Sun* finally broke the story about how the Union Pacific was nearly bankrupt despite record profits on its balance sheet.

The kicker: people were "shocked." The House merely censured Ames. No one lost their jobs and no one went to jail when these bastards carried out this colossal fraud on the American people. After all, they might have been price gouging, but they did actually *build* a transcontinental railroad!

On the other hand Ames didn't live long enough to truly profit from his shenanigans. He died in 1873 at age sixty-nine.

"When the greatest railroad of the world binding together the continent and uniting the two great seas which wash our shores, was finished, I have seen our national triumph and exaltation turned to bitterness and shame by the unanimous reports of three committees of Congress—two of the House and one [of the Senate]—that every step of that mighty enterprise had been taken in fraud."

—George F. Hoar

★40★
WILLIAM ADAMS RICHARDSON
Incompetent Like a Fox
(1821–1896)

"An honest but hopelessly incapable Secretary of the Treasury."
—Edward Atkinson about William Adams Richardson

Because the eight years of Ulysses S. Grant's presidency was one of the most scandal-ridden in American history, we are *still* talking about his administration in this chapter. In this case the bastard in question was an incompetent political hack put into a relatively powerless position where he could safely draw a salary without doing any real harm, only to find himself unexpectedly promoted, costing the government millions of dollars, and losing what reputation he had left.

Ladies and gentlemen, meet William Adams Richardson.

Richardson grew up in Massachusetts with the connections and credentials of a well educated, thoughtful man. He studied at Harvard and even served for several years as a professor at Georgetown's School of Law. Yet, if you believe the man's own words he was at best woefully naïve. And if you don't believe him, he was most likely an outright crook. If his association with one John Sanborn is any indication, he certainly was a terrible judge of character.

Richardson was originally named assistant secretary of the treasury in 1869, the same year that Grant took office as president. When Grant nominated Richardson's boss for a slot on the Supreme Court, Richardson became the treasury secretary. He quickly proved himself hopelessly inadequate for the post.

Richardson ordered the treasury to print more money just after Grant appointed him. In the years after the Civil War the economy expanded so quickly that banks began to grow skittish about having too much of their money out in loans. The more loans that were called in, the more the supply of cash money shrank. Richardson's answer was to get more money (in this case $26 million) into the economy in order to avert a crisis.

But he hadn't consulted anyone, let alone Congress, which technically controlled the federal purse strings. Although Congress eventually chose to overlook Richardson's presumption in this instance, his actions set him up for close scrutiny when the Sanborn Incident came to light.

The lesson to be taken from the so-called Sanborn Incident is that if you're going to sign a contract, you ought to read it first.

Signing any and all contracts drawn up between the treasury and its civilian contractors was one of Richardson's many duties as secretary. Intending to privatize the collection of tax revenue, Richardson expanded the roles of non-government employees hired by the treasury. He employed one such contractor, an out-and-out rogue named John D. Sanborn, to collect $417,000 in back taxes (mostly on liquor sales).

Most private collectors working under such a contract for the Treasury Department were awarded a ten percent commission on whatever they recovered. Sanford's contract called for him to receive fifty percent. Over the course of his contract Sanford raked in $213,000.

When confronted with this chicanery, Richardson claimed that he had thought the contracts pro forma, and had signed them unread. This lame excuse worked for a while. What only came out much later was that Sanford had in turn signed a personal services contract with an assistant, to whom he paid the majority ($156,000) of the money he'd kept.

What was that "assistant's" name? William Adams Richardson, the treasury secretary!

Of course it goes without saying that he resigned. It also goes without saying that President Grant, while personally blameless, provided his loyal friend another job: a slot on the federal bench with the U.S. Court of Claims. Before his death in 1896 Richardson went on to serve as chief justice of that body.

So Richardson went to court, but not as a defendant. Instead he went as a judge, and a wealthy one at that.

Bastard!

BENJAMIN H. BRISTOW
Breaking the "Whiskey Ring"
(1832–1896)

"There has been much talk of late of the fraudulent whisky traffic in the west. If the Secretary wants to break up the powerful ring which exists here, I can give him the name of a man who, if he receives the necessary authority and is assured of absolute secrecy about the matter, will undertake to do it, and I will guarantee success."
—*St. Louis Democrat* owner George Fishback to then–U.S. Treasury Secretary Benjamin Bristow

After inept and corrupt Treasury Secretary William A. Richardson resigned his seat under fire in 1874, the public demanded change. The public outcry over Richardson's many misdeeds moved President Ulysses S. Grant to appoint a man with a spotless reputation in his place. Grant got just that man, and in the end far more than he bargained for, in Benjamin H. Bristow.

Bristow was a Kentucky-born lawyer and Union Army war hero with a solid reputation. As a federal attorney in Louisville, Kentucky, after the Civil War, he enforced the unpopular Federal Civil Rights Acts without letup. This strong commitment to reform helped shape his career.

From 1870 to 1872 Bristow served as the first solicitor general of the United States. In 1873 Congress considered him as a possible successor for Attorney General George H. Williams, who was up for chief justice of the U.S. Supreme Court. But Williams did not become chief justice, and Bristow was out of a job. He went back to the practice of law until Grant tapped him to take over the treasury.

Bristow wasn't in office for long before he got wind the so-called "Whiskey Ring." Several of Grant's appointees had created a complex and sweeping scheme to skim liquor tax profits and share them amongst a group of alcohol distributors and revenue agents. Bristow quickly realized that Grant's loyalty to his office holders threatened his integrity as president, so Bristow decided to act without telling either Grant or Attorney General Edwards Pierpont about his plan.

A BASTARD OF A MONEY-MAKER

Internal Revenue agent John McDonald first hatched the Whiskey Ring scheme. The Bureau of Internal Revenue (the predecessor of the IRS) had sent McDonald to St. Louis in 1870 to collect liquor taxes. McDonald soon realized that there was money to be made from skipping the part where he actually charged the standing seventy-cent federal tax on booze. Instead, he quickly went into business offering distillers and distributors the opportunity to pay less-per-barrel in bribes than they would in taxes. Both greed and politics motivated McDonald's scheme. McDonald was a Republican Party loyalist bent on seeing Grant reelected, and he and his cronies set up the Whiskey Ring in St. Louis and several surrounding cities to acquire off-the-books money for Grant's reelection campaign. As with the other scandals running rampant during his administration, Grant was not complicit in this.

Bristow hired outside investigators to break up the Whiskey Ring, sent over one hundred of the Ring's members to jail, and recovered over $3 million in stolen tax money.

Ironically, President Grant himself proved to be the biggest obstacle to Bristow's crackdown on the Ring. When Bristow indicted Grant's personal secretary Orville E. Babcock as a Ring conspirator, Grant began to interfere. He made sure that Babcock's lawyers had access to prosecution documents to which they had no legal right, giving them a competitive edge.

So Babcock got off. As soon as the Whiskey Ring had been wholly crushed, Bristow resigned in disgust at Grant's actions. He was an early favorite for the 1876

Republican presidential nomination, but lost out to the eventual election winner Rutherford B. Hayes. In 1878 Bristow moved to New York, founded a law firm, and never again served in public office. He died in 1896.

> *"Mr. Bristow I never would have supported [for the 1876 Republican Presidential Nomination for reasons that I may give at some other time in more formal manner than mere conversation."*
>
> —Ulysses S. Grant

★42★

WILLIAM BELKNAP
How Your Dead Wife Can Get You Impeached
(1829–1890)

> "[This Congressional Committee has] found at the very threshold of their investigations uncontradicted evidence of the malfeasance in office by General William W. Belknap . . . Secretary of War."
> —Hiester Clymer

Had enough of the Sewer-Which-Was-the-Grant-administration yet? Well, here's its last entry in our list of bastards: Secretary of War William Belknap.

Belknap, a lawyer by trade, had known Grant since the early days of the Civil War. As a Union Army General, he served with distinction under the future president in such battles as Shiloh. Later in the war, he marched through Georgia to the sea with William Tecumseh Sherman in 1864.

But as distinguished as he'd been on the battlefield, Belknap turned out to be another of Grant's many "friends" who did his administration more harm than good.

Belknap's profiteering came to light by the end of Grant's second term. The secretary of war had taken well over $20,000 in bribes in exchange for awarding no-bid contracts for trading posts in all of the United States's Indian reservations and western frontier forts. Belknap resigned early in 1876, and any talk of a possible third term in the White House for the still-popular Grant went out the door with him. (As ludicrous as that possibility might seem today, there was no constitutional limit on how many times someone could be elected to the presidency until the late 1940s.)

However, if Belknap thought that quitting would end the scandal over his tenure as war secretary, he was mistaken. His conduct had so enraged the members of the House of Representatives that they took an unprecedented step: they voted unanimously to impeach an office-holder who had already resigned. Belknap was also tried in the Senate, where the required two-thirds majority to convict was not reached.

But the net result was the same, and Belknap was out.

BASTARD'S WIFE

Belknap's ill-fated bribery scheme wasn't actually his idea: he inherited it from his second wife Carrie. As secretary of war, Belknap oversaw contracts to place trading posts in Indian reservations and western frontier forts. When Belknap entered office in 1869, all of those contracts expired, including the one at Ft. Sill in the Oklahoma Territory. Carrie hinted to family friend Caleb P. Marsh of New York that if he applied for the concession contract, she would make sure that her husband approved that application—for a price. Marsh, in turn, contacted the previous owner, cut him in on the scheme, and offered to let him continue to run his own trading post on the reservation as a sort of "sub-contractor." The fee was a yearly bribe of $12,000 that Marsh split right down the middle with Carrie Belknap. When she died later that same year, Marsh began sending her cut—in quarterly installments—to her widowed husband. Belknap let the deal play out, happy for the extra income. He eventually married a *third* time. During Belknap's Senate trial it came out that he also let his third wife in on the scheme, making no effort to hide these ill-gotten gains from her. Makes you wonder what conversations around the Belknap dinner table must have been like!

Of course, he did no jail time and didn't even lose his license to practice law. He moved to Philadelphia for a couple of years while his legal situation "cooled off." Belknap eventually returned to Washington, D.C., and continued to practice law until his death in 1890.

Bastard.

★ 43 ★
CONGRESS, PART I
The Salary Grab Act
(1775–)

> "In my many years I have come to the conclusion that one useless man is a shame, two is a law firm, and three or more is a congress."
> —John Adams

No collection of American bastards would be complete without the inclusion of Congress. There are plenty of worthy individual congressmen and senators discussed in this book, but the actual institution deserves credit for its singular bastardry.

During its two-hundred-plus years in existence, Congress has been both witness and party to myriad acts of villainy. Roger Griswold started a fistfight on the House floor with Matthew Lyon and became the first (but hardly the last) member of Congress to face charges of ethics violations in 1798. Preston Brooks savagely beat Charles Sumner in his Senate chamber seat in 1856. The examples seem as endless as they are by turns fascinating and horrifying.

But rarely has Congress been as jointly and starkly self-serving as it turned out to be in 1873 when it passed the so-called "Salary Grab Act." They drafted, voted on, and passed this piece of legislation, alternately known as the "Back-Pay Steal" in the middle of the scandal-plagued administration of President Ulysses S. Grant. In retrospect, it seems as if Congress might have thought that the public would be too distracted to notice a little bit of voting to give the senators and representatives some "well-earned back-pay." After all, Grant's troubles were piling up one on top of the other: the stock market crash, the drying up of ready credit, the Sanborn Contracts, the Whiskey Ring, and a host of other ills. Turns out that Congress could not have been more wrong. Here's how it happened.

In March 1873, Congress entertained a bill calling for a pay raise for the president and all of the members of the U.S. Supreme Court. This in and of itself was unremarkable even in light of the generous raises included. The chief justice was given $10,500 per year, and each of the associate justices was offered $10,000 per year. The president's salary doubled from $25,000 per year to $50,000 per year. Today those salaries would be worth ten times those dollar values when adjusted for inflation. And the public supported both of these portions of the measure in question.

Things hit a snag when the members of Congress tacked a little bonus onto this bill for themselves. They decided that each member of both the Senate and the House ought to also receive a raise from $5,000 to $7,500 per year. Imagine being able to establish your salary with a simple majority vote!

While this was somewhat unsavory, it wasn't illegal. Then Congress decided that its individual members deserved payment for their hard work during the previous two years. They voted themselves the difference ($5,000) between their previous salaries and what they would make after the new raise as a reward for all their "hard work" during the last Congressional session.

The public outcry was deafening. For nearly a year congressmen tried to justify their self-awarded big cash bonuses to their constituents.

By January 1874, though, many members of Congress had begun to fear for their seats in the coming elections. Members of both houses voted overwhelmingly to rescind the portion of the Salary Grab Act that paid them the bonus for the previous years' work. This time the bastards actually listened to the will of the people and lost!

★44★
ANDREW CARNEGIE
"Conscience Money" in Action
(1835–1919)

"We accept and welcome, therefore, as conditions to which we must accommodate ourselves, great inequality of environment, the concentration of business, industrial and commercial, in the hands of the few, and the law of competition between these, as being not only beneficial, but essential for the future progress of the race."
—Andrew Carnegie

If ever there was someone who demonstrated the notion of "conscience money," it was Andrew Carnegie. At one point the country's richest man, Carnegie eventually donated most of his massive fortune to the charitable foundation that still bears his name today.

And why did he do this?

Guilty conscience.

Andrew Carnegie was born poor in Dunfermline, Scotland. His family immigrated to the United States, settled in Ohio when he was thirteen, and he spent his youth even poorer than he had been back in Scotland. Determined to better his prospects, the young Carnegie worked hard, invested shrewdly, and made the most of his opportunities. His investments in a railroad sleeping car company were especially lucrative. By the time he was thirty at the close of the Civil War, he was a millionaire.

During the Civil War, Carnegie had contracted for the War Department and was able to see the writing on the wall for his future investments. He positioned himself to profit immensely from the post-war commodities boom, especially in oil, coal, and eventually (to the exclusion of nearly all other investments) in steel production. Put most succinctly, Carnegie did not make most of his money from shrewd investment, or by making his companies competitive. He and his fellow bastard robber barons Henry Clay Frick, Jay Gould, J. P. Morgan, and John D. Rockefeller stifled competition to the point of forming monopolies in growing industries. Thus they gained enough power to set the price at will of the commodities they controlled Carnegie's good of choice: steel.

He succeeded in part by keeping operating costs low. That meant that he needed to keep labor costs low. So Carnegie certainly had no love for labor unions—the groups of workers intent on reversing or at least slowing the growing distance between the incomes of the rich and poor. Carnegie proved a clever bastard on this point. He did not take on the unions or associated social reformers directly and even expressed shock and dismay when associates like Frick did so viciously during the 1892 Homestead Plant strike.

Instead, Carnegie publicly pledged to work with the masses and then secretly used his wealth and influence to sabotage those negotiations. He managed to keep the government out of the business of taxing and regulating businesses; he was a particularly strong opponent of wage and price controls.

Carnegie also worked to keep his operating costs low by using a revolutionary public relations campaign that foreshadowed those of such later corporate philanthropists as Microsoft founder Bill Gates. The rich, Carnegie said, were intended to be stewards of wealth, and as such had a moral (but not a legal) obligation to help serve and elevate the poor. "A man who dies thus rich," Carnegie wrote in his 1889 book *The Gospel of Wealth*, "dies disgraced."

By 1901 Carnegie's conscience had begun to get the better of him. He allowed financier Morgan to put together a buy-out deal wherein Carnegie received $435 million (worth around $4 billion today) for selling his company. He instantly became the wealthiest man in the country. By the time he died eighteen years later, Carnegie had given away close to $300 million of his conscience money. He even paid for the creation of hundreds of libraries from bricks to books.

Still a bastard.

> *"Surplus wealth is a sacred trust which its possessor is bound to administer in his lifetime for the good of the community."*
>
> —Andrew Carnegie

HENRY CLAY FRICK
Everything but Plagues of Locusts
(1849–1919)

"We bought the son of a bitch and then he didn't stay bought!"
—Henry Clay Frick on Theodore Roosevelt

Imagine a robber baron so ruthless that he was able to shock a bastard like Andrew Carnegie. That's Henry Clay Frick.

Born and raised in western Pennsylvania, Frick got into the steel business early, founding his own coke-producing company (coke is an element that helps get blast furnaces hot enough to make iron into steel) before he was twenty-one. By the time he turned thirty he had bought his partners out.

Frick formed a decades-long business partnership with millionaire steel-magnate Carnegie after a chance meeting while Frick was honeymooning in New York City. He eventually merged his interests with Carnegie's to form U.S. Steel Corporation.

Frick was directly responsible for the devastation associated with the Johnstown Flood of 1889. He and several wealthy cronies had banded together as the South Fork Fishing and Hunting Club and had ordered an earthen dam built on a tributary creek of the Conemaugh River, just a few miles upstream from Johnstown, Pennsylvania.

In May of 1889 the dam failed due to shoddy maintenance (and heavy rains), and the city of Johnstown was wiped off the map. The flood killed over two thousand people and caused millions of dollars worth of damage. Frick's lawyers succeeded in keeping Frick and the rest of the "club" from paying a dime in restitution.

Frick is probably most notorious for his response to the Homestead Steel Strike in 1892 (which in turn appalled Carnegie so much). When strikers took over the Homestead Plant during an impasse in talks between Frick's company and the steelworkers' union, Frick bypassed local law enforcement and hired three hundred

Pinkerton detectives to take back the plant by force. Several people were killed in the ensuing bloodbath. After regaining control of the plant Frick fired two thousand employees (regardless of whether or not they had played any role in the strike) and halved salaries for the few who managed to keep their jobs. For Frick it was an unqualified success: he'd broken the union and actually made money doing so.

BASTARD BY APPOINTMENT

Frick had so much pull with the various Republican presidential administrations during the late nineteenth century that he would use them to help him attempt to get rid of troublesome business rivals in a unique manner. He'd get the rival appointed U.S. ambassador to a foreign country! And not in the third world, either: in 1897 Frick got President William McKinley to offer the post of ambassador to Switzerland to John George Alexander Leishman in order to get him to resign as president of United States Steel. The next time Frick tried this stratagem it didn't work so well. He got James Hazen Hyde appointed U.S. ambassador to France in order to try to get Hyde off the board of his father's insurance company. When Hyde refused the post, Frick had to settle for smearing him in the press as a spendthrift who misappropriated funds from the company.

Toward the end of the strike an anarchist named Alexander Berkman broke into Frick's office intending to kill him. He shot Frick twice in the neck and stabbed him four times before being overpowered and arrested. Frick was back at work within a week, and Berkman went to jail for twenty years.

Due to be deported in 1919 as a result of his ongoing anarchist activities, Berkman at least had the satisfaction that the bastard who he blamed for so much misery had died before he could be forced from the country. Frick was dead of a heart attack at age sixty-nine.

"[Frick was] deported by God. I'm glad he left the country before me."
—Alexander Berkman on hearing of the death of Henry Clay Frick

★46★

J. P. MORGAN
International Banker and Millionaire
War Profiteer
(1837–1913)

"Capital must protect itself in every way . . . . Debts must be collected and loans and mortgages foreclosed as soon as possible.
When through a process of law the common people have lost their
homes, they will be more tractable and more easily governed by
the strong arm of the law applied by the central power of leading
financiers. People without homes will not quarrel with their leaders. This is well known among our principle men now engaged
in forming an imperialism of capitalism to govern the world. By
dividing the people we can get them to expend their energies in
fighting over questions of no importance to us except as teachers
of the common herd."

—J. P. Morgan

John Pierpont Morgan's wealthy banking family raised him to appreciate the value of
a dollar. Where people were always disposable to Morgan, capital was quite another
matter. And like Secretary of War Simon Cameron, Morgan was a war profiteer.
And it wasn't as if he needed the money he stole. Morgan was born rich!

Morgan grew up sickly, receiving the majority of his education in Europe. He
joined his father's organization by going to work in the bank's London office in 1857.

During the American Civil War, Morgan and a partner saw an opportunity to
make a real (literal in this case!) killing. They bought a batch of cast-off, defective
rifles as surplus scrap metal from the U.S. Army, had the guns retooled, and then

turned around and sold the rifles back to the Army. The price per gun when Morgan and his partner bought them: $3.50. The price at which the two men sold these defective guns back to the Army: $33.00! When the guns exploded upon firing— doing greatest harm to most of the soldiers who used them—federal officials realized that they had been re-sold their own defective firearms. They refused to pay, and Morgan went to court (TWICE!) to try to get his blood money.

HOLIDAY BASTARD

Morgan's uncle, James Lord Pierpont, was a famous composer of his day. His biggest moneymaker was the time-honored classic *Jingle Bells*, which he originally entitled *One-Horse Open Sleigh*. Northern-born, Pierpont lived in Savannah for most of his adult life, served in the Confederacy during the Civil War, and by all reports rarely ever saw snow after his childhood. It's hard to connect the hard-nosed founder of The House of Morgan with something as light-hearted as a classic Christmas carol!

Of course it goes without saying that Morgan, like so many rich men during the period, couldn't be bothered to do his patriotic duty to his country during its hour of need. Morgan paid a substitute to serve in the Army in his place, as did fellow bastards John D. Rockefeller and Grover Cleveland. Makes you wonder whether that substitute ever came to any harm because of his rifle exploding, doesn't it?

PHILANTHROPIC BASTARD

If you've ever enjoyed the exquisite art displayed at the Metropolitan Museum of Art in New York City, you likely have Morgan to thank for that pleasure. He donated much of his private collection near the end of his life to help seed the current world-class collection at the Met. Apparently the tax incentives were too good to pass up.

Morgan went on to broker numerous important deals, including the one that made Andrew Carnegie the wealthiest man in America. He died in 1913 with a personal fortune estimated at over a billion dollars in today's money. The beneficiaries of his philanthropy included Harvard Medical School and the American Museum of Natural History.

That doesn't make him any less of a bastard, or of a war profiteer, for that matter.

"How did Mr. Morgan get this mortgage on his native land?"
—*Watson's Magazine*

47

RUTHERFORD B. HAYES
The Stolen Election of 1876
(1822–1893)

"[Rutherford B. Hayes is] a third rate nonentity, whose only recommendation is that he is obnoxious to no one."
—Henry Adams

Imagine that, as a citizen, you've just endured eight years of the most corrupt, venal, and self-seeking government in recorded history; for those who are not fans of George W. Bush, it won't be too much of a stretch to get in touch with that feeling. Now further imagine that after those forgettable eight years in our country's history, the election intended to sweep the previous pack of liars, incompetents, and thieves right out of office is stolen, keeping the offending political party firmly in power.

At least the Bushies had the "decency" to swipe a contested victory at the *beginning* of their boss's eight years in office. President Ulysses S. Grant's administration just kept on sullying elections and politics right through both of his terms. It ought to come as no surprise that his party (the Republicans) just couldn't leave well enough alone when it came to the election of 1876.

For what it's worth, the Democrats were no better. The party then out of power worked desperately to swing the election in favor of their candidate, former New York Governor Samuel J. Tilden. One Democratic governor, Lafayette Grover of Oregon, even refused to certify an elector who was going to vote for Republican presidential candidate Rutherford B. Hayes. The state of affairs began to unravel from there.

Four states—Florida, Louisiana, South Carolina, and Oregon—had "irregularities" with their electoral votes thanks to charges of fraud and corruption. What's more, Colorado had so recently become a state that there was little time to organize actual polling there; the state's legislature awarded all three of their electoral votes to Hayes.

In the end, Tilden won the popular vote; he beat Hayes with just over 250,000 votes. But he lost the electoral count by a single vote: Hayes garnered 185 to Tilden's 184.

For the first time in American history the clear winner of the electoral vote had failed to win the popular vote. At least in 1824 when Andrew Jackson had won the popular vote, the five candidates split the electoral vote and Jackson won a plurality.

Congress finally fixed the situation with a classic back-room deal. The Democrats agreed to accept Hayes if he would in turn recall the Union troops who had been propping up Reconstruction Republican state governments in the South since the end of the Civil War. Hayes agreed and sold Tilden down the river. The civil rights advances of Southern ex-slaves under Reconstruction went right along with him.

The ordeal of the election of 1876 and its aftermath broke Tilden's health. He accepted his loss with admirable restraint and retired from public life.

Hayes was such a pious man that he made the nation wait an extra day for him to take office as president, because the original inauguration date was set for a Sunday. Yet this "Godly" man, so upright and honest, made a political deal that ensured that the disenfranchisement of African Americans would continue in parts of this country for nearly a century after the end of the Civil War.

Pious bastard.

"My task was to wipe out the color line, to abolish sectionalism; to end the war and bring peace . . . I am reluctantly forced to admit that the experiment was a failure."

—Rutherford B. Hayes

48

GROVER CLEVELAND
Producing His Own Bastard
(1837–1908)

"Ma, Ma, Where's My Pa? Gone to Washington, Ha-Ha-Ha!"
—Political chant used by Grover Cleveland's electoral opponents

Successful former judge, lawyer, businessman, and mayor of Buffalo, Stephen Grover Cleveland was a picture of Gilded Age virtues and stability; he was also the only man elected to two nonconsecutive terms as president of the United States. And yet this paragon dodged the draft, had a child out of wedlock, and eventually married a much younger woman for whom he was serving as legal guardian.

Extramarital sex has been a part of the human experience since the invention of the institution of marriage. In the nineteenth century, America was smack-dab in the middle of the so-called "Victorian Age," with its supposedly more stringent approach to morals. But really it was no more moral than at any other point in history. The difference was that personal immorality and vice were less likely to be acknowledged or even discussed then than they are now.

Could a character like Cleveland actually have won the most recent election? Take a good look at the recent implosion of John Edwards's political career after the revelations regarding the kid he had with a member of his campaign staff. Now answer the question for yourself. How can anyone explain the fact of Cleveland's successful election not once, but twice? Especially when he didn't win as a favored incumbent the second time?

First: all voters in presidential elections before 1920 were male. Men tended to wink and nod at each other over situations such as the one in which Cleveland found himself.

Second: there was no such thing as a paternity test in those days, and it's likely the little boy that Cleveland acknowledged as his son wasn't even his. The woman who bore the child "dated" several different men at the same time, Cleveland among them.

Where Cleveland differed from the rest of this young woman's "boyfriends" was that he was the only one of them who was still unmarried. So it seems that Cleveland "took one for the team." He paid for the child's upbringing and apparently received help in that endeavor from the rest of the "circle of male friends" the child's mother had cultivated. Never mind that the boy also happened to be named after Cleveland's married law partner and was apparently the spitting image of him.

WHAT'S IN A BASTARD NAME?

What kind of guy changes his name from "Stephen" and opts instead to use his middle name of "Grover" instead? "Steve Cleveland" became "Grover Cleveland" for no recorded reason. One name sounds like the sort of guy you can have a beer with. The other sounds like that of the pompous-ass president of a bank somewhere.

As for dodging the draft, Cleveland was the sole supporter of his widowed mother and sisters when the American Civil War broke out. At the time it was legal for someone drafted for military service to hire a "substitute" who could serve in his place. Cleveland opted for that, and his political opponents made him pay for it for the rest of his life.

And speaking of Cleveland's law partners and orphaned daughters, Cleveland's law partner Oscar Folsom named the future president as his daughter Frances's guardian in his will. The child was eleven years old when her father died. Cleveland had known the girl since her birth and bought her first baby carriage as a present. After Folsom's death, Cleveland took an active role in supervising Frances's upbringing, including seeing to it that she went to college. At some point his feelings for her changed, and he proposed marriage even though he was executor of her father's estate. She accepted. They were married right after her twenty-first birthday, and had five children together.

Grover Cleveland, upright Victorian gentleman.

"Though the people support the government, the government should not support the people."

—Grover Cleveland

49

JOHN D. ROCKEFELLER

"The Octopus"

(1839–1937)

> "Competition is a sin."
> —John D. Rockefeller

Born and raised in upstate New York and the suburbs of Cleveland, Ohio, John D. Rockefeller was mild-mannered and an avid churchgoer who neither smoked nor drank during the entirety of his long life. The son of a God-fearing mother and a wastrel father, Rockefeller learned much from the examples of his parents. His mother instilled in him a strong work ethic and a deeply religious and moral streak. His father showed him what happened to people not willing to work hard; several of his businesses failed before the younger Rockefeller was out of his teens.

Rockefeller got the message. No one during his long life ever called him "lazy."

On the other hand Rockefeller did not confuse his personal Christian morality with business ethics. He and his nineteenth century robber baron contemporaries were convinced that "capitalism" and "competition" were mutually exclusive. Rockefeller and his peers profited mostly by eliminating competitors, not by outselling them.

Rockefeller made the majority of his money in oil. By 1895 he controlled (directly or indirectly) ninety-five percent of the world's oil reserves. In the 1870s, he wiped out the competition in Cleveland and formed Standard Oil Corporation (muckraking journalists dubbed it "the Octopus"). Like Wal-Mart today, he was able to command a pretty hefty discount in his shipping costs because he ordered and sold goods in such bulk.

Mere discounts didn't satisfy him for long. Rockefeller decided that he wanted to pay even less than the cut-rate that his main hauler, the Pennsylvania Railroad, was charging him at the time. So he bought his own railroad and went into business against them. In turn, the Pennsylvania Railroad tried to compete with Rockefeller. His former partners on the railroad board purchased several oil refineries and began producing their own oil.

But Rockefeller was indeed the Wal-Mart of his day. He bought out the oil production interests of his railroad competitors and forced them to sign contracts charging him far below the actual cost of carrying his oil. Things just got worse after this for the owners of the Pennsylvania Railroad; Rockefeller's draconian contracts and steep profits eventually forced them to fire thousands of employees in order to make ends meet.

By the 1890s, Rockefeller had become the wealthiest man in the world. He was the first billionaire in history, and he controlled most of the oil production on the planet. Is it any wonder that reforming President Theodore Roosevelt targeted Rockefeller's Standard Oil? Though he labeled it an anti-competitive "trust" operating as a monopoly and worked to dissolve Rockefeller's power, Roosevelt didn't succeed in breaking up Standard Oil during his presidency. But he did get the wheels moving. What he began during his administration *was* completed in 1911 when the U.S. Supreme Court found Standard Oil in violation of the Sherman Anti-Trust Act and ordered its dissolution.

Rockefeller even made a killing in the resulting stock sell-off. Worse still, he lived to be nearly one hundred, rich till the day he died, even though—as he had his entire life—he continued to give ten percent of everything he earned to his church.

Late in life Rockefeller followed in Carnegie's footsteps and began to donate more and more of his vast fortune to philanthropic causes. Rockefeller money almost singlehandedly built the University of Chicago.

As if that makes up for all of the misery the guy caused in the interim!

"One of the most depressing features . . . is that instead of such methods arousing contempt, they are more or less openly admired. . . . There is no gaming table in the world where loaded dice are tolerated, no athletic field where men must not start fair. Yet Mr. Rockefeller has systematically played with loaded dice . . . . Business played in this way loses all its sportsmanlike qualities. It is only for tricksters."

—Ida Tarbell

★50★

WILLIAM LORIMER
The "Blond Boss of Chicago" Bribing His Way into the U.S. Senate
(1861–1934)

"When they call the roll in the Senate, the Senators do not know whether to answer 'Present,' or 'Not guilty.'"
—Theodore Roosevelt

William Lorimer was born in England and emigrated to Chicago as a boy. He had little formal education, but he could have earned a PhD in the workings of inner-city politics. He lost just two elections during his long career; it's said that he never won any one of them fairly. Lorimer was nothing if not a typical boss of the times: a machine politician and ward heeler in the tradition of New York's Tammany Hall who helped pave the way for Chicago's formidable twentieth century Daly Machine.

After moving to Chicago with his family in 1870 young Lorimer jumped into union organizing, real estate, and eventually, politics. He built both his career and his machine on his ability to deliver votes to politicians and his knack for landing public jobs for the illiterate urban poor in return for those votes. Lorimer's loyal constituents elected him to Congress as a Republican for four terms between 1894 and 1902, even though he had few qualifications for governing. The *Chicago Tribune*'s editorial board pointed this out in an Op-Ed piece it ran on Lorimer: "He knows considerable about carrying primaries, but he knows no more about political, industrial, or social subjects than does a hole in the ground which doesn't care what goes down it."

If any of this fazed Lorimer he didn't show it. Instead he ran in 1909 for what would one day become Barack Obama's U.S. Senate seat. Since U.S. Senators were still elected by state legislatures at this point, Lorimer only needed to influence about a hundred people to vote for him. So he did what came naturally.

He bribed them.

When word of Lorimer's payoffs for the Senate seat broke out in the press, the Senate focused an intense investigation on the contentious election results. The inquiry's resolution and subsequent debate did nothing to hide the ugly truth: "Corrupt methods and practices were employed in his election, and that the election, therefore, was invalid." The Senate then put teeth to its resolution (a rarity if ever there was one) by reversing the election results. Lorimer plagued every Republican Party member he could think of for assistance, protested in the Senate, and pleaded with President William Howard Taft. But it was all for naught. The Senate officially removed him on July 13, 1912.

BASTARD'S AMENDMENT

Lorimer's purchase of a U.S. Senate seat so outraged the public that Congress responded by passing the Seventeenth Amendment to the U.S. Constitution and instituted the direct election of U.S. Senators by the voters. There had previously been periodic attempts at this sort of reform, but it took the Lorimer scandal to galvanize the Senate into changing the way we elect senators.

Lorimer returned home to a hero's welcome in Chicago, where he attended a public meeting sponsored by his political machine, and literally wrapped himself in the American flag. He denounced reform-minded newspapers like the *Chicago Tribune*—the ones who spearheaded the investigation into the ways of his machine. Lorimer claimed that his foes were corrupt and that he was blameless. Ending the speech to thunderous applause, Lorimer vowed to return to national office at the next opportunity.

He never did. Instead he founded a bank that failed within a couple of years. Later he tried to wheedle a resource development deal with the Colombian government in the 1920s. He failed in that attempt too. He died in Chicago in 1934.

And it goes without saying that he never spent a day in jail.

"(Lorimer) cost us a lot of money, but he is worth it."
—Chicago political fixer Edward Hines

★51★

WOODROW WILSON
Enlightened President and Just Another White Southern Racist
(1856–1924)

> **"The white men were roused by a mere instinct of self-preservation . . . until at last there had sprung into existence a great Ku Klux Klan, a veritable empire of the South, to protect the Southern country."**
> —Woodrow Wilson in *A History of the American People (1901)*

Was there ever a more thoroughly educated American president than Thomas Woodrow Wilson? Holding a bachelor's degree in history from Princeton and a PhD in history and political science, Wilson also studied law for a year at the University of Virginia. He was a political progressive and a reform-minded Democrat. Yet this most "enlightened" of presidents also managed to be a bigoted racist who turned a blind eye to civil rights abuses in his own back yard.

Wilson was born in Virginia right before the Civil War and raised mostly in North and South Carolina. Had he billed himself differently, his attitudes about race would not be all that shocking in light of the age and region in which he grew to manhood. But Wilson portrayed himself time and again as an "idealist," not a traditional schemer of a politician. America was, as he would state in one speech, a singular nation of high values:

> *"Sometimes people call me an idealist. Well, that is the way I know I am an American. America, my fellow citizens—I do not say it in disparagement of any other great people—America is the only idealistic nation in the world."*

After all, this is the man whose idealism brought America into World War I; he was the same man who went to Paris to negotiate the Versailles Treaty. The pact was intended to end that war, and Wilson's "Fourteen Points" program was supposed to prevent war by ending its causes: tyranny, economic imperialism, and so on. Wilson's fingerprints were all over the resulting document.

But Wilson's hands were also all over problems with race back home. From 1913 when Wilson took office to 1919—the year he went to Paris—the number of blacks working in federal jobs slid steeply. This was no accident.

CHANGEABLE BASTARD

Wilson wrote his doctoral dissertation on the failures of the American political system. According to Wilson the weak, scandal-ridden presidential administrations of the Gilded Age had failed to rein in Congressional excesses for a decade (think Ulysses S. Grant). Wilson claimed that this era of political fraud led him to the conclusion that the United States needed to scrap its Constitution. He wanted to trade it for a British-style parliamentary government. Wilson changed his mind after fellow bastard Grover Cleveland's administration reasserted the powers of the executive branch.

Many of the men Wilson nominated for his cabinet were like him: white, Southern, and deeply hostile to blacks and the notion of civil rights for all. As soon as they took office, members of Wilson's cabinet began segregating their departments. The separation included restrooms and drinking fountains, even though the offices had been integrated since the Civil War. When a group of black civic leaders visited Wilson to bring this to his attention and register their disapproval, Wilson shrugged off their complaints, saying that re-segregating federal service would eradicate "the possibility of friction" among federal employees.

With so many progressive reforms to Wilson's credit, including the Federal Reserve Act, farm subsidies and banking reforms, it's hard to reconcile his concern for working people (especially the working poor) with his antipathy toward blacks. However, this is the man who once termed the black vote "ignorant and hostile" toward white people and blacks themselves "an ignorant and inferior race." Many beliefs from America's early years appear bigoted in light of today's more egalitarian notions, but even allowing for changing racial attitudes over time these are the words of a bitter racist.

And that makes progressive, "enlightened" Thomas Woodrow Wilson a bastard.

"[D]amned Presbyterian hypocrite!"

—Theodore Roosevelt

★52★
HARRY M. DAUGHERTY
U.S. Attorney General and All-Around Thief
(1860–1941)

"I've often wondered myself."

—Harry M. Daugherty in response to a reporter's question: "Why have more crazy stories been told about Harding's administration than of any other man ever elected President?"

Harry M. Daugherty was a member of Warren G. Harding's "Ohio Gang" and U.S. Attorney General from 1921 to 1924. His time in the Attorney General's office was the most scandal-plagued in history up until the tenure of Alberto Gonzales. And Harding knew from scandal. Between his own rampaging libido and the thieving natures of the men he appointed to serve under him, his administration was riddled with as much controversy as the Grant administration.

~

BASTARD WHITEWASH
After he retired from practicing law in 1932, Daugherty wrote a book intended to clear his name. In it he claimed that his bagman/boyfriend Smith had killed himself because of failing health and that Albert Fall became interior secretary only by forging Daugherty's signature!

Daugherty was an Ohio lawyer who ran most of Harding's campaigns after the turn of the century and helped engineer his nomination for the presidency in 1920. In return Harding appointed Daugherty attorney general; Daugherty didn't waste any time cashing in.

Word quickly got out in the Justice Department that Daugherty was open to bribes in return for favorable treatment. He was also involved in that largest and farthest-reaching of the Harding administration scandals, Teapot Dome. But Daugherty really made his name and his money through his "bagman" Jess Smith.

Smith served as an unofficial assistant to Daugherty, but his real job was to keep the president's women quiet about their extramarital affairs after Harding tired of them. Smith proved adept at "handling" Harding's castoffs, and Harding valued him for it.

IMPEACHING THE BASTARD

Once open for business Daugherty quickly ran afoul of congressional reformers bent on impeaching him for fraud. He had made a fortune by selling off property seized from German citizens during World War I; the proceeds of these sales made their way back to his bank account. Daugherty was slick though, and he covered his tracks well. There was no way to tie him directly to the money he'd made because he had his bagman (and boyfriend) Jess Smith to serve as his fall guy.

Eventually Smith and Daugherty were rumored to be co-conspirators in the influence-peddling business. They also shared rooms in Washington, D.C.'s Wardman Hotel and whispers pegged them as gay lovers. But the truth was hard to confirm. Whether or not they were involved with each other, Smith *was* linked to a cash payoff from bootleggers seeking immunity from arrest and prosecution under the Volstead Act (the law that kicked off Prohibition in the United States). His position as a conduit soon became common knowledge, but Daugherty's identity as the true recipient of all this bribe money was kept a secret. Within a year of taking office as attorney general, Daugherty had even launched "investigations" into cases of purchased power in the Harding administration. These inquiries always came up empty, and Daugherty just got richer.

His influence didn't protect Smith from everything. Authorities not tied to his Justice Department boss started closing in on Smith. With threat of prison looming large, Smith committed suicide in 1923. Daugherty later wrote of his "roommate": "I never recall this man without a heartache. I knew him in life as a loyal, lovable friend and good fellow. And I have not yet found it possible in my heart to think evil of him."

As for Daugherty, he hung on as attorney general until replaced by Harding's successor, Calvin Coolidge, in 1924. Twice tried and never convicted on charges of fraud related to his time in office, Daugherty returned to Ohio and practiced law until dying in bed in 1941 at the ripe old age of eighty-one. He never spent a day in jail.

53

WARREN G. HARDING
Getting Hard in the White House Phone Booth
(1865–1923)

"An army of pompous phrases moving across the landscape
in search of an idea."
—William McAdoo describing the speeches of Warren G. Harding

Warren G. Harding was far and away the least competent chief executive this country had during the twentieth century (Dubya doesn't count. He belongs to the twenty-first century). In fact Harding was even worse than any of the mediocrities who camped out at the White House during most of the nineteenth century. He was the ultimate product of corrupt machine politics: Harding was handsome, outgoing, and not too bright. He was a back-room glad-hander and dealmaker who got his start by marrying the daughter of the richest man in his small Ohio hometown. And while he wasn't much of a "policy guy," Harding was definitely good at *being* a U.S. Senator. At the time he just needed to be himself!

DEATH OF A BASTARD

Harding's wife was reading to him when he died, and rumors quickly began to spread that the Duchess had mudered Harding. Gossips claimed that she had poisoned the president rather than allow him to face trial on corruption charges alongside so many of his cabinet members. Mrs. Harding refused to allow her husband's body to be autopsied, and that only fed theories that she had a hand in his death.

When Harding's machine got him elected first as a U.S. Senator and then as president, he didn't arrive at the White House friendless. He took with him such thieving members of the "Ohio Gang" as his poker buddies Harry M. Daugherty and Albert Fall. He also brought his penchant for card playing, cigar smoking, and skirt chasing. Harding's wife—a formidable woman whom he nicknamed "The Duchess"—always suspected her husband of fooling around behind her back and used to stalk through the halls of the Executive Mansion looking for him.

In order to dodge her, Harding used to meet his "secretary"—a buxom, curvy blonde named Nan Britton—in the cloakroom that President Theodore Roosevelt had converted into the first phone booth in the White House. Apparently it was the only place in the entire mansion where the Duchess didn't think to look for Ol' Warren.

BASTARD IN A CHINA SHOP

Warren G. Harding once ran out of cash while playing cards in the White House and wound up gambling away all of the White House china in an attempt to reverse his losing streak! Washington socialite Alice Roosevelt Longworth later described the "ambiance" in Harding's Executive Mansion poker games as follows: "the air heavy with tobacco smoke, trays with bottles containing every imaginable brand of whiskey, cards and poker chips ready at hand—a general atmosphere of waistcoat unbuttoned, feet on the desk, and spittoons alongside." Never mind the fact that these games took place during Prohibition: the booze the president and his cronies were drinking was illegal!

Then the inevitable happened: Harding sired a child in the room. (Britton wrote about it several years after his death, in a book titled *The President's Daughter*.) Harding's handlers gave Britton $100,000 in hush money and sent her on a cruise around the world.

Shortly before his death, Harding began to get wind of all of the grafting taking place. The potential for scandal began to worry him. While traveling west on a summer tour in 1923, Harding asked his secretary of commerce (and future president) Herbert Hoover for his two cents: "If you knew of a great scandal in our administration, would you for the good of the country and the party expose it publicly or would you bury it?"

Hoover, a very honest fellow, responded that in such a case he would expose the scandal. Harding never made up his mind what to do about it. He died of a heart attack in San Francisco later that same summer.

54

ALBERT FALL
Teapot Dome and the Original "Fall" Guy
(1861–1944)

"I have no trouble with my enemies, I can take care of my enemies all right. But my friends, my goddamned friends, they're the ones who keep me walking the floor at nights!"
—President Warren G. Harding

Everyone knows the term "fall guy." He's the person who will take the blame and consequences of someone else's criminal act, even if it's murder. This poor soul may not even know the criminal; he may simply be getting "framed" and is otherwise blameless. But where did the term originate? Meet the original "fall guy": former Senator and Interior Secretary Albert Fall of New Mexico. He was a far-from-blameless man involved up to his eyebrows in one of the greatest bilking schemes of the twentieth century: the Teapot Dome scandal.

Fall settled in New Mexico while it was still a territory, began to practice law there, and jumped feet first into local politics. Fall was a fixer, a guy who got deals done. He also represented and got off several notorious gunmen accused of murder, including one for the death of Fall's longtime political rival. Fall became a senator when New Mexico became a state in 1912. During his nine years in the Senate, Fall allied himself with Ohio Senator Warren G. Harding and his followers.

Elected president in 1920, Harding appointed Fall secretary of the interior. Fall then persuaded Navy Secretary Edwin Denby that the Interior Department should manage the Navy's huge oil reserves inside the United States like Buena Vista, California, and Teapot Dome, Wyoming. Fall immediately leased these deposits for a ridiculously low price to two old friends from his early days in New Mexico: Henry F. Sinclair and Edward L. Doheny. He didn't bother allowing for bids on the oil leases (a violation of federal law). In return Fall received a $100,000 cash "loan" (worth over $1 million today) from Doheny's son. Doheny immediately became the wealthiest man in the country.

Too much money and too many people were involved in the swindle for it to remain a secret, and *The Wall Street Journal* broke the story about the "loans" to Fall on April 14, 1922. Sloppy before this story broke, Fall managed to cover his tracks afterward. By the time the Senate named a subcommittee to investigate, Fall had made everything look perfectly legal.

BASTARDS BY ASSOCIATION

Fall's co-conspirators Sinclair and Doheny hardly escaped the scandal scot-free. Sinclair tried to bribe the jurors in his trial and went to jail on a contempt charge. He wound up having to sell his Fifth Avenue French Renaissance-style mansion in New York City as a result. Doheny spent a fortune on a crack legal defense team and got off. To add insult to injury, he later foreclosed on Fall's New Mexico ranch for failure to repay the $100,000 "loan" with which he had been bribed. But Doheny paid too. On February 16, 1929, the son who had handed off the $100,000 bribe to Fall feared that federal investigators were closing in on him; he shot his best friend and manservant (who had also been present when Fall took the bribe), then turned his gun on himself.

When Montana Senator Thomas J. Walsh uncovered the "loan" Doheny's son had hand-delivered, Fall and Denby were quickly forced out of office. In 1927 the Supreme Court invalidated the original leases; by this time, however, millions of barrels of oil had been pumped out of these lands at an immense profit for Sullivan and Doheny. In 1929 Fall was convicted on bribery charges and spent a year in jail; he was the first cabinet-level government official in American history to do so. He died broke in El Paso, Texas, in 1944.

★55★
HUEY LONG
The Kingfish
(1893–1935)

"No man has ever becn President of the United States more than two terms. You know that; everyone knows that. But when I get in, I'm going to abolish the Electoral College, have universal suffrage, and I defy any sonofabitch to get me out under four terms."
—Huey Long

Huey Long's picture ought to be next to the word "demagogue" in the dictionary. The irony is that Long didn't start out that way. He started out as just one more little guy trying to help other little guys.

A middle child in a large Louisiana family, Long's elder siblings were able to go to college; by the time young Huey was of age to consider an higher education, however, the cost of college had skyrocketed. The luxury was well beyond his middle-class, farm-owning family's means, even though he'd won a scholarship that would have taken care of his tuition. Instead Long went to work as a traveling salesman, peddling everything from medicine to canned goods to books.

During this time he discovered that he had the common touch. A born politician, Long had a way of ingratiating himself with people almost immediately.

In the interim he attended college here and there, and after just one year at Tulane Law School he convinced the local bar association to allow him to take the bar exam. He passed it, and was admitted to the Louisiana Bar in 1915. He immediately went into private practice, mostly working for poor clients suing large companies.

By 1922 Long had been elected chairman of Louisiana's Public Service Commission; representing that entity he sued Cumberland Telephone & Telegraph for price gouging. He won, and forced a settlement that called for CT&T to reimburse over 80,000 of its ratepayers a total of nearly $440,000. This made him quite popular with the poor and middle class, and Long ran unsuccessfully for governor in 1924.

He ran again in 1928 with the campaign slogan "Every man a king, but no one wears a crown." As part of his program, Long promised voters services many of them had never envisioned before, including paved roads to replace the dirt ones that turned into red clay muck during the Gulf Coast's rainy season. This time he won.

Long immediately set about redistributing Louisiana's wealth mostly at the expense of its oil companies. He taxed the big corporations at ever-higher rates and cut the taxes of what he called "the rest of us." All the while he increased services for the poor, including supplying free textbooks to schoolchildren and state-sponsored night adult literacy courses. This cemented Long's power-base with lower and lower–middle class voters.

And the people loved him as much as his growing list of enemies among the rich and intellectuals loathed him. But at some point for Long it became about power, and not about the people he served.

After two years as governor, Long ran for the U.S. Senate in 1930 without resigning his seat. He won, and was sworn in to the Senate in 1931, still without resigning his seat. Long held two posts for over a year: he was both the governor of Louisiana and the state's U.S. Senator. Not since John Marshall had served as both U.S. Secretary of State and U.S. Supreme Court Chief Justice had anyone done that.

Long emerged as a critic of Franklin D. Roosevelt, announcing as early as 1934 that he intended to make a primary challenge of FDR in the 1936 election. He never got the chance. A doctor whom Long had smeared by claiming he had "coffee blood" (a euphemism for being mixed-race) shot Long dead in the Louisiana State Court House on September 8, 1935.

> *"[Huey Long] is not a fascist, with a philosophy of the state and its function in expressing the individual. He is plain dictator. He rules, and opponents had better stay out of his way. He punishes all who thwart him with grim, relentless, efficient vengeance."*
>
> —Raymond Gram Swing in *The Nation*, January, 1935

★56★
HARRY S. TRUMAN
The "Senator from Pendergast"
(1884–1972)

"My choice early in life was either to be a piano player in a whorehouse or a politician. And to tell the truth, there's hardly any difference."
—Harry S. Truman

The world knows President "Give 'Em Hell" Harry Truman for his blunt speech, forthright manner, and historic endeavors. He used an atomic bomb to end World War II, faced down the Soviet Union at the beginning of the Cold War, integrated the U.S. Armed Services, and won reelection in the most stunning upset in American political history.

He was also a machine politician connected throughout his career to one of the most corrupt "kingmakers" in American history.

Truman had been a failure as a farmer and as a haberdasher. He seemed the most unlikely of political hacks, but he needed help to get into the game. So Truman called on Kansas City political machine boss Tom Pendergast. He backed Truman's run for the comparable position to a county commissioner's seat in eastern Missouri. Pendergast exerted his powerful influence on Truman's career for the next two decades, and helped the young man rise through the ranks. Though he rejected Truman's desire to run for Congress or the governorship at first, Pendergast got him elected as a U.S. Senator from Missouri in 1934. Truman won by a large margin, but had trouble getting meetings with President Franklin Delano Roosevelt, who airily dismissed the Missourian as "the Senator from Pendergast."

In spite of his reputation as a machine politician, Truman carefully built up his reputation for honesty. He let Pendergast choose the people Truman would appoint and support in government jobs (this was known as Truman's "patronage"), but made it clear that Pendergast never influenced his congressional votes. Keeping it that way wasn't easy. Political machines would sink hooks into politicians who could serve their interests. The poor chump would arrive at a hotel room for a "meeting" and find young women waiting for him. Whether or not any hanky-panky went on, if the sucker got caught, then the machine had leverage against him.

BASTARD FUNERAL
When Pendergast died on January 26, 1945, newly sworn-in Vice President Truman attended his funeral—the only elected official to do so. When asked by a reporter what he was doing there, Truman spoke with characteristic bluntness: "[Pendergast] was always my friend and I have always been his."

Truman never forgot this. He was a devoted family man and was never linked to any of the "other women" stories that so often crop up in the closets of prominent politicians. Late in life, Truman was asked how he was able to avoid even the hint of bad behavior in an age where politicians kept mistresses the way modern campaign managers keep opinion polls; Truman was as forthcoming as ever. The key, he said, was never to allow himself to be caught dead in a room alone with a woman not related to him. Not only would he walk out of a room in which a woman was alone, he made a point of getting up and walking out of *any* room into which a single woman was sent—even if he was to be there with other men. And it worked.

Pendergast helped fix one too many elections, and in 1939 the newly elected Missouri governor (who owed his new office to Pendergast) threw the boss under the bus. Pendergast went to jail and his political machine was broken. Pendergast was finished as a machine politician, and he lived out the rest of his life in a quiet Kansas City suburb. Truman, so careful to keep clean and clear of the fray, was never even questioned about his relationship with Pendergast.

★57★
STROM THURMOND
Racist in Public; "Integrationist" Behind Closed Doors
(1902–2003)

"I wanna tell you, ladies and gentlemen, that there's not enough troops in the army to force the Southern people to break down segregation and admit the nigra [sic] race into our theaters, into our swimming pools, into our homes, and into our churches."
—Strom Thurmond in a speech given while running for the presidency as a "Dixiecrat" in 1948

Remember Thomas Jefferson, the great sage and enlightened thinker who secretly fathered several children with one of his slaves? Or Woodrow Wilson, the enlightened president who was also not so secretly a bigot?

Well, meet James Strom Thurmond, a noxious combination of the two. The Southern racist supported segregation well into his sixties. And apparently Thurmond wanted to keep the races separate because he was afraid that more white people might do what he had done himself: have children with black people.

Thurmond grew up in a family of well-to-do farmers in South Carolina. In 1925, shortly after he graduated college at Clemson, Thurmond fathered a daughter with the family's fifteen-year-old maid, Carrie "Tunch" Butler. The baby's name was Essie Mae Washington.

Thurmond sent Essie to live with relatives of her mother in Pennsylvania, but she had no idea who her father was until the late 1940s, when her mother took her to secretly meet Thurmond in Washington, D.C. Thurmond never publicly acknowledged his daughter. Instead he paid for Essie's upkeep and education. He put her through school and helped her become a teacher as he had briefly been before turning to politics. Thurmond and Essie met many times. She later recalled that she attempted to talk to him about his antediluvian views on segregation in Southern society on several occasions. Thurmond, the same man who owns the record for the length of a filibuster by a single senator (at just over twenty-four hours) while singlehandedly trying to block the Civil Rights Act of 1957, didn't have much of an answer. He brushed off her questions, saying that it wasn't personal.

HEROIC BASTARD

Like so many bastards before and since, Thurmond was an honest-to-goodness war hero. He served in the U.S. Army during World War II and was decorated for bravery a number of times. He received both the Bronze Star and the Purple Heart during his career, and he was honored for the day he landed at Normandy in a glider with other members of the 101st Airborne Division. He rose to the rank of Lt. Colonel before the end of the war.

After all, Thurmond was the poster boy for segregation. He led a coalition of conservative Southern Democrats embittered by President Truman's racial integration of the U.S. Armed Forces after the war and Truman's attempts to rid the country of racially motivated "poll taxes." Thurmond became the presidential candidate of these "Dixiecrats"—known officially as the States Rights Democratic Party—in the election of 1948. Thurmond received thirty-nine electoral votes and won four states, all of them in the Deep South.

As the Democratic Party continued to become more liberal over the course of the twentieth century, Thurmond felt more and more out of step with the party. He crossed the aisle and joined the Republican Party in 1964. He served in the Senate continually from 1956 until shortly before his death in 2003. During that time he moderated his views on race, but never once acknowledged his biracial daughter Essie.

Perhaps he didn't think the time was right. Perhaps he didn't think people would understand. Perhaps he felt he'd done the best he could.

But surely the man who stormed ashore in Normandy on D-Day didn't fear public opinion. Thurmond lived to be one hundred. By the time he was in, say, his seventies, and his daughter in her fifties, he had made a career for himself several times over. What, really, was there left to fear?

★58★
ALLEN DULLES
Defying the Popular Will
(1893–1969)

> "From an early age [Dulles] set out to make people like him. Affability, he discovered, was a most useful character trait."
> —Peter Grose

The grandson, nephew, and brother of three different U.S. secretaries of state, Allen Dulles felt from an early age that he was born to make a difference. This former Wall Street lawyer and diplomat had starkly contrasting sides. He was, by turns, engaging and cruel; he was possessed of rock-solid moral certitude and a habitual womanizer. And as director of the CIA from 1953 to 1961, he betrayed everything he supposedly stood for.

At Dulles's behest, the CIA in the 1950s toppled two legitimate, democratically elected governments; coups d'état brought down and replaced Iranian Mohammed Mossadeq and Guatemalan Jacobo Árbenz Guzmán. And the most relevant question is "why?" Simple: the specter and threat of potential nationalization.

Both Iran and Guatemala had long histories of serving as economic colonies of the West. In Iran's case the British Empire had exploited its vast oil reserves and paid the Iranian government a mere sixteen percent of the *net* profits it enjoyed.

By the 1950s the Iranian economy was so bad that President Mohammed Mossadeq considered nationalizing Iran's oil industry. Though the change would save Iran, it would also effectively cut the British off from their sweet profits and force them to pay fair market prices for their oil and gas. The British sought and got the help of the CIA. Mossadeq was denounced by a ruthless and well-funded propaganda organization as a despot who had misled the electoral process. Just like that, he was ousted, and the son of a British-deposed shah took over Iran.

In Guatemala's case the bone of contention was land. An American corporation called the United Fruit Company owned most of the land in the country in the early 1950s, as it had for decades. United Fruit had a long history of interfering in the internal affairs of Central American countries, and the corporation frequently requested and received assistance from the U.S. government. United States troops intervened in the interest of keeping United Fruit's operating costs as low as possible. These low costs included the bribes that greased corrupt Guatemalan government officials into agreeing that United Fruit should only have to pay about $3 per acre in taxes on "unimproved" tracts of land. Of course, the land was actually worth many times more than that.

So when Jacobo Árbenz Guzmán was elected president of Guatemala in 1951, he decided to nationalize the company's holdings in his country. He seized the land and goods, and redistributed them to the peasants so that they could feed themselves. To add insult to injury, Guzmán even offered to reimburse United Fruit, but only at the rate at which they had valued their lands for the purpose of taxation assessment: $3 per acre!

That was the beginning of the end of Guzmán. Both Dulles and his brother secretary of State John Foster Dulles, were major stockholders in the United Fruit Company; when corporation officials went to them in a panic, Dulles acted with alacrity. Within months the CIA had been called in and backed yet another coup of an elected leader. By 1954 their efforts had (pardon the pun) borne fruit. This time the deposed president fled into exile in Mexico and was replaced by a military junta willing to continue to "tax" United Fruit at the agreed-upon $3 per acre.

Bastards.

"Perhaps we have already intervened too much in the affairs of other peoples."
—Allen Dulles

★59★
RICHARD J. DALEY
The "Last Boss"
(1902–1976)

"I'm not the last of the old bosses. I'm the first of the new leaders."
—Richard J. Daley

The "last boss" was the guy who delivered the 1960 presidential election to John F. Kennedy; he was the man who ordered out riot police and asked for help from the Illinois National Guard to suppress protestors picketing the 1968 Democratic National Convention in Chicago. The "Last Boss" Richard J. Daley once said that there was no partisan way to ensure that the garbage got picked up on time. He would have known. No one—not even gangsters like Al Capone—so completely controlled the levers of power in the Windy City before or since Daley took office in 1955.

Daley was one of the last of the machine politicians that defined big city politics in America throughout much of the late nineteenth and early twentieth century. Born in the shadow of the stockyards on Chicago's infamous South Side, Daley went to law school at night while working as a clerk. Although he briefly hung out his shingle in 1933, Daley's career was in politics.

Daley worked his way up through the city's ward system. When he first ran for office in 1936, he won a seat in the Illinois House of Representatives as (of all things) a Republican. A lifelong Democrat, Daley switched parties only so he could get elected, and quickly switched parties again in 1938 when he was elected to the Illinois State Senate.

For the next seventeen years Daley held a succession of posts. He learned the ropes and forged alliances that helped him build a power base within the Cook

County Democratic Central Committee. In 1953 he was elected its chairman. Two years later he became Chicago's mayor, a post he would hold for the rest of his life.

During his formative years as an Irish-American politician, Daley made friendships and political alliances with like-minded Irish-Americans across the country. The most prominent of these was Joseph Kennedy of Massachusetts.

When Kennedy's senator son John ran for president in 1960, Old Joe Kennedy depended on Daley to help bring Chicago, and by association the rest of Illinois, to his son's electoral tally. Daley did deliver, to the everlasting outrage of the Republicans, by stuffing the voting roll sheets with thousands of names taken from the city's cemeteries. All of the forged ballots safely "voted" for Kennedy and the rest of the Democratic Party ticket. Kennedy won Illinois by eight thousand votes.

When Chicago was tapped to host the 1968 Democratic Party National Convention, Daley intended to use the national stage to showcase how well his machine ran the city. He forgot to consider the "Yippies" and their allies in the Antiwar Movement. Their protests began spinning out of control on August 23, 1968.

Fearing that anarchy would result from this raft of demonstrations, Daley okayed the use of force in shutting down the dissenters, including orders to shoot to kill anyone caught with a gun. Things got heated and eventually the governor called out the Illinois State National Guard to help restore order.

Daley didn't lose his office, but he did pay a price politically. As his power base eroded, Daley's health also began to decline. In 1976 he died suddenly as a result of his second heart attack in as many years at seventy-four. According to many historians, Daley's time in office wasn't without benefit for his constituents. He worked to renew Chicago's downtown and made its walking suburbs livable and attractive to the city's middle classes; Daley's work kept them (and their tax dollars) from fleeing the city limits for the suburbs as they had in nearly every other large American city over the past two decades.

"Fuck you, you Jew son of a bitch, you lousy motherfucker, go home."
—Richard J. Daley to Connecticut Senator Abe Ribicoff after Ribicoff questioned Daley's using riot police during the 1968 Democratic National Convention

JOE MCCARTHY
America's Witch-Hunter-in-Chief
(1908–1957)

> "Have you no sense of decency, sir? At long last, have you
> left no sense of decency?"
> —Joe Nye Welch

No book on the subject of "bastards" (political or otherwise) would be complete without the inclusion of that opportunistic train wreck "Tailgunner Joe" McCarthy, Republican senator from the state of Wisconsin from 1947 to 1957. A falsehood-spewing, grandstanding gasbag of the first order, McCarthy's meteoric rise to public celebrity was equaled only by his precipitous fall from grace.

Born on a Wisconsin farm in 1908, McCarthy dropped out of school while very young to help work the family farm. At age twenty he completed the entire local high school curriculum over the course of a single year, then went to college and settled on the law as a vocation. By 1938 he had passed the bar and gotten himself elected to a nonpartisan judgeship.

McCarthy joined the Marine Corps at the outset of World War II, and was immediately commissioned as an officer because of his status as a judge. He served in a noncombat role with a Marine aviation unit as their intelligence officer. By the end of the war he had earned the rank of captain.

After the war McCarthy prepared to run for the U.S. Senate and lied his ass off about his war record in furtherance of his political aspirations. He succeeded in getting elected as a senator from Wisconsin in the 1946 elections and maintained a low profile for his first three years in the Senate.

All that changed in a February, 1950, speech given at Wheeling, West Virginia: McCarthy claimed that the State Department was riddled with Communists, many of them spies. Over the next four years McCarthy set out on a witch hunt, seeking to rid first the federal government and then the entertainment industry of people who might be either spying for or sympathetic to the Soviet Union. With the Cold War just starting, people were frightened. The time was ripe for the rise of a demagogue willing to play on that fear to his advantage.

BASTARD B.S.

Among the many lies McCarthy told were that he had enlisted at the beginning of the war and that he had flown thirty-two combat missions, thereby earning consideration for the Distinguished Flying Cross. He later received the honor based upon more falsifications in his paperwork; he claimed he had broken a bone in his foot as a result of being shot down, but it actually happened during a hazing ceremony on a troop ship headed to the South Pacific.

In speech after speech, McCarthy went after "secret Communists" and "Soviet agents" that always seemed to be just around the corner. And although his allegations were invariably filled with bombast, they were equally light on proof.

McCarthy's fall was just as spectacular as his rise. In 1953 he began investigating rumors of a spy ring that reportedly infiltrated the U.S. Army. In these "Army–McCarthy Hearings," McCarthy met his match in Army lead counsel Joe Nye Welch. He also made a fatal mistake: he allowed the proceedings to be recorded for a documentary film. He came across as a bully. It all came to a head when the soft-spoken, unassuming Welch (who seemed downright fatherly on TV) called America's Witch-Hunter-in-Chief out:

> *Until this moment, Senator, I think I have never really gauged your cruelty or your recklessness. Fred Fisher is a young man who went to the Harvard Law School and came into my firm and is starting what looks to be a brilliant career with us . . . I like to think that I am a gentle man, but your forgiveness will have to come from someone other than me.*

> *And that was that.*

His power broken, McCarthy continued to serve in the Senate, but his political career was over. The bully had been faced down. Within three years he was dead of hepatitis at the age of forty-eight.

Bastard.

"Senator McCarthy's zeal to uncover subversion and espionage led to disturbing excesses. His browbeating tactics destroyed careers of people who were not involved in the infiltration of our government."

—Senators Carl Levin (D–Michigan) and Susan Collins (R–Maine)

★61★
JFK
"Fiddle and Faddle"
(1917–1963)

"It was the best thirty seconds of my life."
—Actress Angie Dickinson joking about her tryst with President Kennedy

He was the movie-star handsome, Harvard-educated, wealthy son of a powerful Massachusetts family. Winner of both the Congressional Medal of Honor and the Pulitzer Prize for Biography. President. Hero. Martyr. Icon.

Womanizer. Plagiarist.

John Fitzgerald Kennedy.

As it turns out Kennedy's Pulitzer Prize–winning book *Profiles in Courage* was largely ghostwritten; most scholars think it was the work of future White House aide Arthur M. Schlesinger, Jr. But it made JFK look intellectually deep, and his father Joe worked hard to get one of his boys elected president and made sure the book got a mountain of publicity.

The fact that Jack Kennedy liked women is well established, and women returned the favor. It's also well-known that his wife was aware of his serial adultery. Once, Jackie even showed him a piece of lingerie left behind by one of his dalliances and asked him to return the item to the lady in question, as it wasn't Jackie's. Kennedy had quite a taste for Hollywood actresses, and had reportedly slept with a number of them including Angie Dickinson, Gene Tierney, and of course, Marilyn Monroe.

Kennedy and Monroe met for the first time when they attended a February 1962 party held in the president's honor at the home of his brother-in-law, actor Peter Lawford. The sparks flew and they quickly began an affair.

She went on solo vacations with Kennedy, and stayed over at the White House while the First Lady was away. And then there was the whole singing "Happy Birthday" thing. Monroe fell in love with Kennedy; he viewed sex as something more along the lines of a tag-team sport. The affair couldn't last, and it didn't.

According to Kennedy confidant Florida Senator George Smathers, Kennedy ended things with Monroe in a particularly callous manner. After a day spent sailing on the Potomac, he told her he wasn't interested in getting a divorce. "You're not exactly First Lady material, Marilyn," he said by way of letting her down.

And that was that.

Monroe's life had already been spiraling out of control for over a decade as a result of the long struggle with her manifold personal demons. Within months of the breakup, she was dead of a drug overdose. What Kennedy felt about her passing is not recorded.

FIDDLE AND FADDLE

It is a well-documented fact that Kennedy was a lifelong and inveterate womanizer. What is not nearly so well-known is the part played in JFK's sex life by a couple of women given the codenames "Fiddle" and "Faddle" by the Secret Service. Both women were attractive and married. Both were on the White House payroll and listed their occupations as "secretary" (although neither of them could type). Apparently both women were highly adept at "helping the president relax." Their special assignment was to join JFK for frequent lunchtime nude swims and accompany him on trips where the First Lady was not in attendance. None of this was reported by a "respectful" White House Press Corps, nearly all of whom were men.

Perhaps the most telling insight into Kennedy's attitudes regarding love, intimacy, and sex has been offered by Frank Sinatra's valet, George Jacobs. He knew Kennedy from the times the president was a guest at the singer's Beverly Hills home. In an interview given long after Kennedy's assassination in November 1963, Jacobs said

"His need was like that of Alexander the Great: to conquer the world. To him, Marilyn was one more conquest, a trophy—maybe the Great White Shark of Hollywood, but still a record, not a romance."

"The great enemy of the truth is very often not the lie, deliberate, contrived and dishonest, but the myth, persistent, persuasive and unrealistic."

—John Fitzgerald Kennedy

LYNDON BAINES JOHNSON
Bathroom Power Politics
(1908–1973)

> "There are no favorites in my office. I treat them all with the same general inconsideration."
> —Lyndon Baines Johnson

Texas-born and hardened in the crucible of the Great Depression, Lyndon Baines Johnson grew up to be both an effective and a quotable bastard. He is known today largely for his role as John F. Kennedy's successor as president of the United States after Kennedy's assassination and for getting the nation embroiled in the unpopular Vietnam War. But Johnson was also likely the most successful majority leader in the history of the U.S. Senate.

Johnson began his political career as an aide in Texas state government, and proved himself capable of rousing people and getting things done. He was elected to the House in 1937 and held office there for twelve years. Johnson spent part of this time in the Naval Reserve during World War II, operating as President Franklin D. Roosevelt's eyes and ears in the Pacific Theatre. He even earned a dubious Silver Star award for observing fifteen minutes of combat time on a B-26 bomber run. In 1949 Johnson moved to the U.S. Senate. During his twelve years there, Johnson rose within the Democratic leadership, taking over as Senate majority leader in 1954 when the Democrats reclaimed the majority.

Johnson was, without doubt, the most effective Senate majority leader ever. He studied the senators working within his caucus and applied the "Johnson Treatment" to the ones from whom he wanted votes. Journalists Roland Evans and Robert Novak described the strategy as a combination of intimidation and cajolery; "an almost hypnotic experience" that "rendered the target stunned and helpless."

He ran for the Democratic presidential nomination in 1960, but lost. Johnson surprised many by accepting the offer to be Kennedy's running mate. Kennedy's staff knew he needed a Southerner on the ticket to land the South's electoral votes that year. Johnson met that goal, and he also (allegedly) assisted in the voter fraud that delivered Texas to Kennedy.

BASTARD IN THE BATHROOM

Power is a funny thing. Like confidence, the appearance of power is often more important than the actuality of it. This is particularly true when trying to get employees to do your bidding without having to constantly threaten or discipline them. Johnson, a student of human nature, chose to remind members of Congress and of his cabinet that he was running the show by sending them to the bathroom. He had a habit of calling government officials who weren't getting their jobs done to see him in the White House. When notified that the subordinate in question was awaiting entry into the Oval Office, Johnson would go into his small private bathroom, drop trow, and make the person sent for discuss the issue while Johnson sat on the toilet. No one ever openly questioned who was in charge during Johnson's administration.

Vice President Johnson was publicly loyal to the president, but behind closed doors, he chafed at the public's love affair with the handsome young Kennedy. "Jack was out kissing babies," Johnson once remarked, "while I was out passing bills."

But when Kennedy was assassinated in November 1963, Johnson hit the ground running. He passed more sweeping social reform legislation than any president since Franklin Roosevelt. Johnson was responsible for so many things we take for granted today including Medicare, Medicaid, and the Civil Rights Acts of 1964 and 1965. These accomplishments, though, did little to save his career.

Johnson also escalated the war in Vietnam, and that cost him the White House in the long run. He retired from politics in 1969 and died in 1973.

★63★
ADAM CLAYTON POWELL, JR.
His Own Replacement in Congress
(1908–1972)

> "A man's respect for law and order exists in precise relationship to the size of his paycheck."
> —Adam Clayton Powell, Jr.

Born in Harlem to an energetic Abyssinian Baptist Church minister, Adam Clayton Powell, Jr. was an impressive man. He, too, was an ordained minister and the first black member of the New York City Council. Powell was also the first black congressman from the state of New York and one of the first from any state in the union since the end of Reconstruction in 1877. In 1937 he succeeded his father in his pulpit and began to work as a community organizer in his home neighborhood.

As such he was a stellar figure. Harlem's personal representative in Congress, a tireless worker for civil rights, Powell insisted that black visitors be allowed to dine with him in the "Whites Only" Congressional dining room and that the use of the word "nigger" be banned on the House floor.

He was also a tireless administrator, chairing the powerful House Education and Labor Committee in 1961. Working with President Lyndon B. Johnson, Powell even set a record for the number of bills to be introduced into legislation in a single session.

And yet Powell ran afoul of House ethics rules. He abused his committee's budget to the tune of funding unauthorized overseas trips for himself. These included weekend getaways to a home he owned in the British Virgin Islands. He was also missing sessions of the committee he chaired. It all looked (and was) highly improper.

By January 1967, the members of the House's Democratic leadership had seen enough. They stripped Powell of his chairmanship; a March 1 session of the entire body voted overwhelmingly to exclude Powell from the House.

Rather than fight his expulsion, Powell ran in the special election organized to pick the replacement for his Congressional seat. He won.

WHAT'S IN A NAME?

Powell was married three times, and had a son with second wife, Hazel Scott, whom they named Adam Clayton Powell III. That son in turn had a son, whom he named Adam Clayton Powell IV. When Powell had a child with his third wife Yvette Diago, they named that boy Adam Clayton Powell Diago. When Powell Diago later ran for the New York State Assembly he changed his name to Adam Clayton Powell IV, even though he already had a nephew by that same name! And speaking of Diago, she moved back home to Puerto Rico in 1961, and lived there full-time until 1967. During those six years she drew a salary as a Congressional aide for her husband, even though she wasn't in the United States and did not work for the congressman.

The House refused to seat him. This time Powell went to court. In its 1969 decision on the case *Powell v. McCormack*, the Supreme Court ruled in his favor, stating that Congress did not have the Constitutional right to exclude him. So Powell went back to Congress, but he lost his seniority. He also went back to skipping sessions, rarely showing up even just to vote.

In 1970 Powell lost a primary challenge to a young Charlie Wrangell, the man who has held Powell's seat ever since, and who himself is no stranger to public controversy. Powell retired to the Bahamas and died in a Miami hospital in 1972. Despite the lackluster end to his Congressional career, Powell is memorialized by (among other things) the Adam Clayton Powell, Jr. State Office, which sits on Adam Clayton Powell, Jr. Blvd. in Harlem.

★64★

ABE FORTAS
Your Personal Supreme Court Justice— for a $20,000 Fee
(1910–1982)

"There's an old Russian saying that you don't roll up your pants until you get to the river. There should be a very comprehensive statement by Fortas. He owes it to the court and the country."
—Former House Judiciary Committee Chairman Emanuel Celler

Abe Fortas had an established career as a star lawyer: after all, he had been the primary attorney in several cases argued before the Supreme Court, including the landmark 1962 case *Gideon v. Wainright*, which established a citizen's right to legal representation. He was also a lifelong friend and confidante of President Lyndon B. Johnson. So when he was confirmed as an associate justice of the Supreme Court in 1965, Fortas seemed to have a long career on the Supreme Court ahead of him. Neither he nor anyone close to him could have foreseen his resignation under fire a short four years later.

This was partly because no justice had ever been successfully impeached for any reason during the long history of the U.S. Supreme Court. In fact, since the Democratic Republicans had gone after Samuel Chase in 1804, no one had even bothered to try. Thanks to Fortas, all of that was about to change.

The first cloud on the horizon came when Johnson nominated Fortas to replace retiring Chief Justice Earl Warren in 1968. During the confirmation discussions in the Senate, concerns arose about a series of speeches that Fortas had given at American University. Fortas had been paid $15,000 for the speeches, but the university had not paid these fees: a number of private corporations had. If these companies ever had a case tried before the high court, Fortas's relationship to them could create a conflict of interest. These concerns helped derail his nomination.

A year later the revelation that he had signed a personal services contract with a $20,000 retainer from the personal foundation of a Wall Street financier was the final blow that finished Fortas's judicial career. The contract called for Fortas to receive $20,000 per year in addition to his retainer for the rest of his life. In exchange for this remuneration Fortas was to give "advice" to the family paying him.

"It was difficult for most people to fathom why Fortas, an astute attorney and author of a recent book that begins 'I am a man of the law,' would so jeopardize his position," A *Time* magazine article noted at the time. "Fortas's many connections in high places have gained him a reputation for wheeling and dealing in areas not uncommon for a corporate lawyer but of questionable propriety for a Supreme Court Justice. One fellow lawyer described Fortas as simply 'avaricious.'"

And that's the really interesting part. It's true that $20,000 was not then and still isn't a small sum of money. But compared to the $150,000 per year that Fortas's law firm paid him before he was tapped for the high court, it's a drop in the bucket.

What's more, Fortas's own wife, also an attorney, was still employed at his old firm and bringing in $100,000 per year herself. It's not exactly as if Fortas needed the extra money. In the end, regardless of what it amounted to, Fortas took the money for the same reason so many other infamous bastards have done so: because he thought he could do it without suffering adverse consequences as a result. Turned out he was half right.

In the end the entire sordid affair amounted to an enormous conflict of interest, and since Johnson had left office that year, he was unable to save his old friend. Already wounded by the American University speakers' fees revelations, Fortas resigned on May 14, 1969.

He spent the next thirteen years until his death practicing law in Washington, D.C.

"Judging is a lonely job in which a man is, as near as may be, an island entire."
—Abe Fortas

★65★

RICHARD HELMS
Perjury as the Price of Honor
(1913–2002)

"Nobody knows everything about everything."
—Richard Helms

Here's a hot one for you: the director of the Central Intelligence Agency was once convicted of perjury, and it was the fault of the president of the United States! The director in question? Career "Company" man Richard Helms. The president? Ol' Tricky Dick himself: Richard M. Nixon.

This is what happened.

Helms was one of the agency professionals who advanced into the Company's upper echelons after the Bay of Pigs debacle gave President John F. Kennedy the excuse he need to purge the "Old Guard" of Allen Dulles and his protégés from the CIA's leadership. In 1963 Helms went to Vietnam and helped overthrow President Ngo Dinh Diem. Within a year he was a deputy director. In 1966 President Johnson appointed him director.

It was no secret that Dick Helms loathed Dick Nixon. After Nixon became president in 1969, Helms spent most of his time trying to keep the agency out of Nixon's way. The president wanted to use them for every political "dirty trick" he could think of to keep his "enemies" under his thumb. When the Watergate scandal broke, Helms successfully kept the CIA from getting sucked into that public controversy as well, refusing to post bail for the Watergate burglars with secret CIA funds.

But Nixon still managed to pull the agency in the direction in which he wanted to go and compromised Helms at the same time. In 1973 Nixon insisted that the CIA assist in a Chilean coup to oust democratically elected, socialist President Salvadore Allende. Helms made sure that the takedown was successful.

By now Nixon infuriated Helms, and the CIA director did his best to keep the Company clear of Nixon's petty wars with the rest of the known world. He clearly realized that Nixon had dug his own grave with Watergate and saw the writing on the wall: that if Helms himself wasn't careful, he could be forced out along with Nixon when his turn came.

So when Nixon suggested later that same year that Helms become the U.S. ambassador to Iran, Helms accepted the nomination and resigned as CIA director. Helms and Iran's ruling monarch, the Shah, had enjoyed a good relationship since their days spent in prep school together. He served as ambassador from 1973 to 1976.

A problem arose when it came to light that Helms had lied under oath while in the midst of his Senate confirmation hearing for his new post. When asked point-blank whether the CIA had assisted in Allende's overthrow that same year, Helms had lied and said no, because the matter was still classified.

In 1977 Helms was convicted of perjury as a result of his testimony before Congress. He considered the conviction a mark of honor, because he'd kept the secrets despite the consequences. His $2,000 fine was paid by friends in the CIA. President Ronald Reagan awarded Helms the Presidential Medal of Freedom in 1982.

Shortly before his death in 2002, Helms did something he'd previously sworn never to do: he wrote his autobiography. In it he broke no new ground and defended his participation in the coup that ousted and killed Chilean President Salvador Allende, as necessary "to preserve the Democratic constitutional system." Never mind the fact that Allende was elected by his own people and that the military goons who replaced him were right-wingers bordering on fascist in their political beliefs.

★66★
DANIEL ELLSBERG
"The Most Dangerous Man in America"
(1931–)

> "We could kill him...."
> —Richard M. Nixon

They say that the ship of state is the only ship that leaks from the top. Perhaps the most famous stateside leaker is Daniel Ellsberg, the RAND Corporation economist who worked on a top-secret government study entitled the "History of United States Decision-Making Process on Vietnam Policy, 1945–1967." Today we know this infamous collection of information as the Pentagon Papers. The disturbing findings revealed over the course of the report's seven thousand pages prompted Ellsberg to smuggle the classified papers out of the office. He then photocopied them and leaked them to the Senate Foreign Relations Committee in 1969. This massive doorstop of secrets revealed the Vietnam War as unwinnable by the very people running it.

WHY THE BASTARD DID IT

Ellsberg got the idea to leak the Pentagon Papers at one of the anti-war events he'd begun to frequent even while still working for RAND Corporation on the study. A draft resister spoke movingly about choosing to go to prison rather than choosing to fight in Vietnam. Inspired by the young man's passion and commitment, Ellsberg realized that if he leaked the study he might be able to help put an end to what he now saw as an unjust and unwinnable war. He felt he faced a similar moral dilemma: choose to go to prison for telling the truth or choose to support the war in Vietnam by staying silent.

Ellsberg didn't stop there. Disillusioned by government and inspired by the anti-war movement, he leaked the Pentagon Papers again two years later—only this time he handed them over to the *New York Times*, the *Washington Post*, and more than a dozen other publications.

All hell broke loose when the *New York Times* published the first install-ment of the study. The media milked the revelations of the Nixon administra-tion cover-ups about the extent of our nation's involvement in the war—up to and including the bombing of Cambodia and Laos. The Nixon administration charged Ellsberg with espionage and fought the media all the way to the U.S. Supreme Court.

POSTSCRIPT

In the wake of the Watergate scandal, all charges against Ellsberg were dismissed. He went on to become a leading antinuclear activist. He was arrested more than sixty times in conjunction with his new cause. Henry Kissinger once called Ellsberg "the most dangerous man in America." And as the creator of The Truth Telling Project, which calls upon all federal employees to expose government lies, he may still be. Traitor or hero? You decide.

The government got an injunction against the *Times* in federal court, but failed to get one against the *Post*. The cases were consolidated and heard by the U.S. Supreme Court as *New York Times Co. v. United States*. In a 6–3 decision, the high court ruled that the injunction against the *Times* violated the First Amendment, ruling that the government failed to show that "grave and irreparable harm" would result were the injunction not granted.

Back at the White House, John Ehrlichman authorized "Hunt/Liddy Special Project No. 1," designed to discredit Ellsberg. On September 3, 1971, about a month after the Supreme Court ruling, G. Gordon Liddy, E. Howard Hunt, and three CIA agents broke into Ellsberg's psychiatrist's office in a vain effort to obtain evidence against him.

Sure, it sounds like something out of a movie. Former hawk risks a life in prison to hand over top-secret documents revealing the Vietnam War as unwinnable to the media, hoping it'll help end the war. But this wasn't a movie. This was real life. And it set the stage for the most devastating of all American political scandals: Watergate.

"We were young, we were foolish, we were arrogant, but we were right."
—Daniel Ellsberg

67

SPIRO AGNEW
Bribery Brouhaha Brings Down Babbling, Bloviating Bastard
(1918–1996)

> "No assassin in his right mind would kill me. They know if they did that they would wind up with Agnew!"
> —Richard Nixon

Spiro T. Agnew was governor of Maryland when presidential nominee Richard M. Nixon picked him to be his running mate in 1968. Republicans gave Agnew the nod because they hoped that a moderate from a quasi-Southern state like Maryland would keep the Deep South happy without alienating Northern voters. In selecting Agnew as his running mate, Nixon extolled the Maryland governor's virtues: "[Agnew] has real depth and genuine warmth. He has the attributes of a statesman of the first rank."

Once sworn in as vice president, however, Agnew quickly lost Nixon's respect. Nixon didn't think Agnew smart enough to be vice president. Nixon's Oval Office tapes reveal that he had thought about kicking Agnew off of the ticket for the 1972 election and replacing him with former Texas governor and then Treasury Secretary John Connally, who had also been governor of Texas earlier in his career. The president and his trusted staffer H. R. Haldeman hatched ingenious plans to dump Agnew, including coming up with the idea of giving Agnew a television station to run.

Agnew saved Nixon the trouble, however. He was forced to resign on October 10, 1973, when he pled no contest to a single charge of tax evasion. It all began with a bribery scandal during his time as the governor of Maryland. As it turned out, Agnew had been taking steady payoffs of nearly $150,000 over a ten-year period while he was governor. He received his last $17,500 "balloon payment" bribe after he was sworn in as vice president! In return for the single plea, Agnew agreed to resign as vice president. Later, a lawsuit filed by a group of George Washington University law students forced Agnew to repay the state of Maryland the nearly $300,000 he took in bribes.

BABBLING BASTARD BLOVIATING BUMPTIOUSLY

As vice president, Agnew claimed to represent the silent majority of Americans who did not protest the Vietnam War. He put two speechwriters—future Republican presidential candidate Patrick Buchanan and future *New York Times* opinion columnist William Safire—to work writing colorful speeches. He attacked his political opponents and many journalists as "pusillanimous pussyfooters" and "nattering nabobs of negativism," among other alliterative epithets. Agnew relished his role as Nixon's "attack dog," giving speeches blasting Vietnam War protesters as "un-American."

Agnew tried to rehabilitate his reputation years later when he published a memoir entitled *Go Quietly . . . or Else*. In the book, he claimed that Nixon and his aides had threatened to have him killed if he didn't resign as vice president. He also claimed to have been framed and that he had never taken a bribe. Released from attorney–client privilege by this claim, Agnew's attorney stated flatly that his client had lied.

After leaving office Agnew moved to California and developed another career as an international dealmaker. He helped oil-rich Arab sheiks acquire foreign business and made millions in the process. He died in 1996.

"Some newspapers are fit only to line the bottom of bird cages."

—Spiro Agnew

68

RICHARD M. NIXON
Impeachable Bastard
(1913–1994)

"Richard Nixon is a no good, lying bastard. He can lie out of both sides of his mouth at the same time, and if he ever caught himself telling the truth, he'd lie just to keep his hand in."
—Harry S. Truman

The dour son of California Quaker parents, Richard Milhous Nixon was born ambitious. During his career he became a congressman, senator, vice president, and successful corporate lawyer. In due course Nixon ascended to the presidency where he cloaked himself in secrecy and suspicion, only to resign the office in disgrace before the end of his second term. In the end he was a victim of his own demons and of the scandal to end all American political scandals: Watergate.

G. Gordon Liddy and E. Howard Hunt, of the White House "Plumbers" unit responsible for stopping leaks to the press, masterminded the break-in at the offices of the Democratic National Committee located in Washington, D.C.'s Watergate office complex on June 17, 1972. The plot was a failure. Then–U.S. President Richard M. Nixon was forced from office when it was revealed that high officials in his campaign organization, the Committee to Re-Elect the President (CREEP), orchestrated the break-in.

A security guard called the police when he found that a door latch had been re-taped open after he had un-taped it. Police arrested five men in the DNC's headquarters. Searches of their hotel rooms revealed thousands of dollars in cash; subpoenas of their bank records turned up $89,000 in donations by the men to Nixon's reelection campaign.

All five men later pleaded guilty to various charges including burglary and wire-tapping; Hunt and Liddy were convicted after a trial and sentenced to prison. One of the burglars, former CIA agent James McCord, implicated White House Counsel John Dean in a letter to U.S. District Judge John J. Sirica. McCord also told Sirica that the burglars pleaded guilty and perjured themselves under political pressure from the White House.

DEEP THROAT

The White House burglars' connection to CREEP was revealed to young *Washington Post* reporters Bob Woodward and Carl Bernstein by an anonymous, shadowy figure named "Deep Throat." The whistleblower's identity was revealed in 2005 to be William Mark Felt, Jr, the associate FBI director in 1972. Felt helped Woodward and Bernstein out after Nixon twice passed him over for promotion to FBI director. According to Felt, one of the Watergate burglars was in possession of checks signed by Hunt and had Hunt in his address book. Ironically, Felt himself was later convicted on charges of civil rights violations connected with a domestic antiterrorism investigation. However, Ronald Reagan gave Felt a presidential pardon at the behest of Attorney General Edwin Meese.

A special prosecutor, Archibald Cox, was appointed to investigate the matter. When he learned that the White House had a taping system installed, Cox subpoenaed the tapes. Nixon refused to provide them, citing executive privilege. He demanded that U.S. Attorney General Elliot Richardson fire Cox. Richardson refused and resigned, as did his assistant, William Ruckelshaus. Eventually Solicitor-General Robert Bork, acting head of the Justice Department, fired Cox.

Leon Jaworski, Nixon's next appointment as special prosecutor, pressed forward with the subpoenas for the tapes. Nixon's claim of executive privilege was ultimately shot down by the Supreme Court.

After Nixon supplied the tapes they were played in court. The smoking gun was revealed on August 5, 1974. A tape dated June 23, 1972—six days after the Watergate break-in—recorded Nixon and White House Chief of Staff H.R. Haldeman discussing how to coerce the CIA director into getting the FBI director to stop the Watergate investigation. Facing certain impeachment and removal from office, Nixon resigned the presidency three days later.

Several of Nixon's aides did jail time as a result of the scandal. Pardoned by Gerald Ford, Nixon never spent a day in jail.

★69★

JOHN CONNALLY
The "Texas Tip"
(1917–1993)

"I got some ideas on Mr. Connally. He ain't never done nothin' but get shot in Dallas. He got the silver bullet. He needs to come back here and get hisself [sic] shot once every six months. I attack Connally on his vanity. He's terribly bad [sic] vain, y'know."
—Bob Bullock

If nothing else John Connally was a survivor. He was a decorated veteran of World War II, successful Texas lawyer, early protégé and longtime ally of President Lyndon B. Johnson, secretary of the navy for President John F. Kennedy, and two-term governor of Texas. Connally went on to switch political parties and serve President Richard M. Nixon as treasury secretary through his administration, including during the height of the Watergate scandal.

By all accounts had Nixon not been worried about a bruising confirmation battle in the Congress, he would have nominated Connally as his vice president when Spiro Agnew resigned in disgrace. In that version of history Connally and not Gerald Ford would have been president after Nixon's resignation. But weighed down by the looming Watergate scandal, Nixon needed someone with Ford's squeaky clean image who could sail through his nomination. With his baggage Connally might have had as much trouble getting confirmed as Agnew had just being vice president.

Oh, and Connally took bribes. Lots of them.

Connally was even captured on some of the White House tapes discussing "oil money" that certain interested parties in Texas would make available for Nixon's disposal should he require it. These tapes would later haunt Connally during his infamous "Milk Money" trial.

In that 1975 scandal, Connally was hauled into court on charges that while working as treasury secretary he took a $10,000 bribe from representatives of the dairy industry. Connally's lawyers managed to suppress the tapes of their client discussing bribe money with Nixon, but only just barely. Connally called a stream of character witnesses from former First Ladies Jackie Kennedy and Lady Bird Johnson to the popular evangelist Billy Graham. He was acquitted.

BLOODY BASTARD

Connally was governor of Texas when he rode in the car with Kennedy on that dark day in Dallas when the president was assassinated in November 1963. Connally himself was wounded in the attack. A sniper's bullet smashed into his back, passed through his chest and wrist, and lodged itself in his thigh. He made a complete recovery, and went on to a long career in politics, most of it as a Republican. When asked in 1982 for a reaction to the Warren Commission's finding that assassin Lee Harvey Oswald had acted alone in killing Kennedy, Connally said, "I do not, for one second, believe the conclusions of the Warren Commission." When asked why he had never said anything about his skepticism before, he said, "Because I love this country and we needed closure at the time. I will never speak out publicly about what I believe."

He" later said of the incident, "To be accused of taking a goddamned $10,000 bribe offended me beyond all reason." The joke around his law office was that Connally was outraged at being accused of taking such an insignificant amount as a bribe; in Texas, they said, $10,000 was considered a "tip."

Connally ran for president in 1980, but his Watergate association made him unpalatable to Republican voters. He lost the nomination to Ronald Reagan. Connally died in 1993 of pulmonary fibrosis (he was a heavy smoker), never having spent a day in jail. He was, however, broke by this time, having been ruined in the S&L scandal of the late '80s.

"When you're out of office, you can be a statesman."

—John Connally

70

WILLIAM CASEY
Iran-Contra's Conveniently Dead Fall Guy
(1913–1987)

> "I pass the test that says a man who isn't a socialist at twenty has no
> heart, and a man who is a socialist at forty has no head."
> —William J. Casey

New York native William J. "Big Bill" Casey was many things over the course of his long life: a World War II–era spy, a '60s-era corporate lawyer, a Republican Party operative, and the head of the CIA during the Reagan administration. Casey likely got away with a campaign "dirty trick" that helped deliver the White House to Ronald Reagan. It is one of history's ironies that he serves in death as the scapegoat that no one had ever succeeded in making him in life.

New York Times columnist William Safire coined the term "Briefingate" for a political scandal without the satisfying conclusion of its Watergate cousin. It started when someone stole materials President Jimmy Carter was using to prepare for the October 28, 1980, presidential debate with his Republican challenger Ronald Reagan. The pilfered briefing book gave Reagan advance notice about the issues Carter intended to cover during the debate. Unsurprisingly Reagan demolished Carter; he painted himself as the better prepared and more at-ease of the two candidates.

The matter did not come to the public's attention until the 1983 publication of Laurence I. Barrett's *Gambling with History: Reagan in the White House*. The revelation caused quite an uproar in the press. The Justice Department interviewed Reagan's senior campaign staff and transition team in response to the resulting public outcry. Michigan Congressman David Stockman, who went on to become Reagan's budget director, admitted using the purloined papers to help Reagan prepare. A later

FBI inquiry turned up hundreds of pages of the documents in Stockman's files and in the archives of the conservative Hoover Institute.

According to Stockman he had gotten the documents from James A. Baker III, a campaign staffer who became Reagan's White House chief of staff in 1981 and treasury secretary in 1985. Baker in turn claimed that he had received them from Reagan campaign manager Casey.

The longtime party operative adamantly denied this allegation. No amount of coercion succeeded in getting the former spy to change his story. Did Baker take the files? Did Casey swipe them? The unanswered questions—which Safire named Debategate—presented the Justice Department with a stone wall. The investigation ran out of steam.

It is important to note that Casey also went on to serve in the Reagan administration, as Stockman and Baker had before him. Some coincidence, huh? Turns out that the guy accused of passing along Carter's debate notes actually had an "intelligence" background dating back to OSS (the CIA's forerunner) service during World War II!

Casey was director of the CIA from 1981 until his death from cancer in 1987. His health began to fail in the years before that, and several longtime friends noted a decline in his mental faculties in the year or so leading up to his death. During the Iran-Contra mess he was posthumously hung out to dry by those involved. Perhaps the sullying of Casey's reputation was warranted, since he was supposedly the linchpin in the whole scheme. Or perhaps it was simply some sort of karmic balancing of the scales for whatever Casey did to get his hands on Jimmy Carter's debate notebook.

Either way the scandal soon lost the attention of the public. After being caught asleep at the switch in Watergate's wake, the media had initially pursued the Debategate story with a vengeance, but dropped it several weeks later. And of course Ronald Reagan suffered absolutely no political fallout as a result of it.

Come to think of it, neither did "Big Bill" Casey. But then again, he was dead.

"The desperate mind that led the Reagan administration over a cliff in his final year at the CIA was not that of the old Bill Casey."

—William Safire

71

ED MEESE
Attorney General as Consigliore, Part I
(1931–)

> "You don't have many suspects who are innocent of a crime.
> That's contradictory. If a person is innocent of a crime, then he is
> not a suspect."
>
> —Ed Meese

Have you heard this one before? The attorney general of the United States—a trusted inner-circle counselor to the sitting president and a cabinet member—runs into some "ethics" problems and gives his notice under political pressure, but he never serves a day in jail for what he did. No, we're not talking about Alberto "Fredo" Gonzales, here. We're talking about Reagan lawyer and later leading light of the Cultural Conservative moment, Edwin "Ed" Meese III.

Meese was born and raised in Oakland, California, the son of a longtime Alameda County treasurer. He finished a stint in the military and graduated law school. Afterwards Meese worked as both a civil attorney and criminal prosecutor before joining the staff of California Governor Ronald Reagan in the 1960s.

Meese served Reagan as legal affairs secretary, executive assistant, and chief of staff before he followed Reagan to Washington D.C. He then became counselor to the president and was on Reagan's National Security Council. While in the White House, Meese, Chief of Staff James Baker III, and Deputy Chief of Staff Michael Deaver were the "Troika," or Reagan's three closest advisors. He became attorney general in 1985 and held that post until 1988.

Although never charged with a crime, Meese was dogged by scandal. Most famous were claims that he had been involved in Iran-Contra and the Wedtech Scandal. Meese's participation in Iran-Contra was shadowy at best, but he managed to cover it up for quite some time. His involvement in the Wedtech Scandal, however, was more personally taxing.

Unlike Iran Contra, this one had Meese's fingerprints all over it. He couldn't account for some "financial improprieties" arising from his tenure as a lobbyist for the Department of Defense contractor Wedtech Corporation. He also couldn't prove that he hadn't participated in "influence peddling" that gave Wedtech a $32 million contract to make engines for the Army, in spite of the Army's conclusion that the company didn't possess the infrastructure or capabilities to produce the engine.

In 1988, Meese resigned after the Justice Department released a report in which he was found "insensitive to the appearance of impropriety." Questions were raised about his failure to file income tax returns showing how much money he actually made from Wedtech.

Meese later served on the Iraq Study Group co-chaired by James Baker and Lee Hamilton. He has called for a return to a "jurisprudence of original intent" by the U.S. Supreme Court. He is also alleged to have subjected judicial nominees to a "litmus test" based on their view of Reagan's policies, most notably abortion. Of course he never spent a day in jail, and continues to be a darling of social conservatives.

How about a litmus test that doesn't allow scandal-plagued former U.S. attorneys general to lecture law-abiding federal judges about their judicial ethics and judgment? Bastard.

"In any other democracy in the world, a Cabinet official who subjected his chief, his party and his cause to the massive embarrassment that Attorney General Edwin Meese III caused President Reagan, the Republicans and the conservative movement last week would be out of a job. He would not have to be asked to resign. He would know it was his simple duty. But in this administration, Reagan neither expects nor enforces any standard of accountability—especially toward such loyal old friends as Meese."

—David S. Broder

★72★

ABSCAM
Congressmen and the Size of Their Pockets

"I did nothing wrong."
—Harrison "Pete" Williams

Sometimes it takes a group to make a proper "bastard." This was surely the case with the group of congressmen looking to line their pockets in what later became the scandal known as "ABSCAM."

It began during the late 1970s as an FBI investigation into allegations of trafficking in stolen property. The FBI set up a shell company called Abdul Enterprises, Ltd.—hence the name "ABSCAM." A Middle Eastern businessman named Kambir Abdul Rahman ostensibly ran the decoy. The FBI set up meetings with public officials claiming that "Rahman" wanted, among other things, to buy assistance moving his money out of his country and asylum in the United States.

The sting netted U.S. Senator Harrison "Pete" Williams of New Jersey; he was later convicted on nine counts of bribery and conspiracy. Williams protested his innocence and appealed his conviction. It got him nowhere. He and all of the other politicians caught up in the ABSCAM investigation were secretly videotaped.

No U.S. Senator (aside from those from Southern states who supported the Confederacy during the Civil War) had been expelled from the Senate since William Blount in 1797. There had been senators since who were threatened with expulsion though, and they had all resigned. Once convicted of a felony Williams's course of action was clear: he resigned from the Senate on March 11, 1982. He served four years in first a minimum-security prison and then a halfway house (on whose board of directors he sat for the rest of his life). Shortly before his death in 2001 Williams petitioned outgoing President Bill Clinton for a pardon. He was rebuffed.

Also convicted of bribery and conspiracy for their roles in the scandal were Congressmen John Jenrette (D–SC), Richard Kelly (R–FL), Raymond Lederer (D–PA), Michael "Ozzie" Myers (D–PA), and Frank Thompson (D–NJ). All five congressmen either resigned or were expelled from office.

Kelly was the only Republican caught up in the sting. He insisted that he had actually spent part of the money he received to keep up a "cover" and that he was taking the bribes to investigate the matter on his own. He was convicted but won a new trial on appeal (the only politician nailed in the ABSCAM scandal to do so), but was convicted again. The videotape of the handoff was particularly damning, as he'd been caught on tape stuffing $25,000 in cash into a coat pocket, then asking one of the men who had just bribed him, "Does it show?"

A fellow Republican, Senator Larry Pressler of South Dakota, refused a bribe on tape, saying, "Wait a minute, what you are suggesting may be illegal." But he also did something about it. Pressler, a decorated Vietnam combat veteran and Rhodes Scholar, then went to the FBI and told them of his contact with the undercover FBI agents. CBS News anchor Walter Cronkite later called Pressler a "hero" on national television.

Congressman John Murtha of Pennsylvania was named as an un-indicted co-conspirator in the scandal and testified against the other defendants. Murtha refused an offer of a bribe on tape, and insisted later that he was seeking potential investment in his struggling Pennsylvania Congressional district.

That sort of "chamber-of-commerce" activity is something every congressman has done at one time or another. Stuffing your pockets full of cash and then wondering whether the resulting bulge ruins the line of your suit, on the other hand, not so much!

"I do not consider myself a hero . . . what have we come to if turning down a bribe is considered 'heroic'?"

—Senator Larry Pressler

★73★
MICHAEL DEAVER
The Medium *Is* the Message
(1938–2007)

"I always imagined that when I died there would be a phone in my coffin, and at the other end of it would be Nancy Reagan."
—Michael Deaver

Michael Deaver was a California lobbyist and political operative in Ronald Reagan's camp. He consulted on Reagan's run for governor of California, as well as his first and second presidential campaigns. Deaver also saved Reagan's life during the 1976 campaign by performing the Heimlich maneuver after the candidate had begun to choke on a peanut.

After Reagan won his second term in 1980, he had to coax Deaver into leaving California to work in his White House. Reagan felt so strongly about having Deaver onboard that he offered him the plum job of deputy chief of staff with responsibility for setting the president's schedule of speaking engagements and attendance at public events, and in charge of overseeing public relations efforts; it was a dream job for a one-time lobbyist with ambitions to be an even more powerful lobbyist *after* his public service was over. It gave him a level of access to the president only enjoyed by the other two members of what the press dubbed Reagan's "Troika" of closest advisors, James A. Baker III and Ed Meese.

As part of the "Troika," Deaver served as White House deputy chief of staff under Chiefs of Staff James A. Baker III and Donald Regan. He became so essential that Reagan compared Deaver's May 15, 1985, departure to start his own lobbying firm to "an amputation." But resign he did and he founded Michael K. Deaver, Inc. Meanwhile, he still received the (confidential) president's daily schedule and retained a White House pass.

Stemming from a March 3, 1986, *Time* magazine cover story, Deaver and his firm came under investigation for violations of the Ethics in Government Act of 1986. The legislation prohibits senior government officials from lobbying the government until two years after their departure. At his trial, Deaver claimed that his alcoholism caused memory blackouts that made him forget calls he made to government officials. The judge overseeing the case, however, barred this defense on the grounds that it was not substantiated by expert testimony. After twenty-seven hours of deliberations, Deaver was convicted of three counts of perjury relating to statements he made regarding lobbying on behalf of TWA, the Republic of South Korea, and Puerto Rico. Originally sentenced to three years in prison, Deaver eventually paid a $100,000 fine, did 1,500 hours of community service, and served three years' probation; of course, he didn't serve a day of his jail sentence.

BASTARD PHOTO-OP

These days, everyone knows what the phrase "photo-op" means. But Deaver coined the phrase "photo opportunity" and used it to supreme advantage getting Reagan's face in front of the public. *Time* magazine called him the "vicar of visuals." Deaver later said of his work: "I've always said the only thing I did is light him well. My job was filling up the space around the head. I didn't make Ronald Reagan. Ronald Reagan made me."

To Deaver's credit he refused an offer of a pardon from Reagan before the president left office. He died of cancer in 2007.

"Looking back, I guess one tip-off was that he really enjoyed the trappings of power. His office contained dozens of photographs, framed in silver, of Deaver with kings, queens, and prime ministers, many of whom he had prevailed on for autographs. There was a lot of the small-town kid from Bakersfield, California, in him, and I suppose he just got carried away with his own importance."

—Larry Speakes

★74★

THE S&LS
A Gang of Rogues

"The banking problems of the 80s and 90s came primarily, but not exclusively, from unsound real estate lending."
—Former Federal Deposit Insurance Corporation (FDIC) Chairman L. William Seidman

As of this writing the memory of the Big Bank Bailout of 2008–2009 was still fresh. The fallout from this whopper of a government spending spree has sparked all manner of public outrage; ordinary citizens often ask jokingly, "Where's *my* bailout?" Banks that have been deemed "too big to fail" have received record amounts of federal loan money in order to stay afloat. Others like Goldman Sachs are already repaying their bailout money and once again handing out absurd payment packages to their highest-achieving traders. Many people who were enjoying the boom times of the early Bush-43–era deregulation of Wall Street banking have had plenty of reason to grouse as they watch their investments dry up. And yet it's not as if this sort of bailout of the improvident rich by the taxpayers hasn't happened before; it actually occurred recently, too.

Ladies and gentlemen, we give you the S&L Scandal of the late 1980s, complete with some very familiar family names!

Prior to the recent Wall Street bank bailouts of 2008 and 2009, the S&L Scandal was the largest taxpayer-funded financial institution bailout in U.S. history. It cost over $160 billion; nearly all of it was borne by the taxpayers. The bailout added to the ballooning budget deficits in the early 1990s; many see it as the main cause of the 1990–1991 recession (and by association, of President George H. W. Bush's election loss in 1992).

US S&Ls (short for "Savings & Loan") were similar to British "building societ-ies." They were nonprofits that primarily, if not exclusively, made mortgage loans to ordinary working people. They were originally called "building and loans" and, in the prewar period, were most popular in the Eastern and Midwestern United States.

MORE BASTARD BUSHES!

The S&L bastard dust-up reads like a veritable *Who's Who of United States Senators and Ne'er-Do-Well Scions of Politically Powerful Families*, and it includes several Bushes! Future Florida governor Jeb Bush defaulted on a $5 million real estate loan; he later paid $500,000 to "settle" it once he'd had the property reappraised. And younger brother Neil Bush was the direc-tor of Silverado Savings and Loan when it failed. The FDIC found that he had engaged in "multiple conflicts of interest," and sued to recover mil-lions of dollars he allegedly "loaned" himself. For his part, Neil Bush main-tained that "self-serving regulators" were going after him because he was the son of the president. He later paid $50,000 to settle the FDIC's lawsuit, a pretty cheap buyout in light of the millions he mishandled while running the repository of so many people's savings into the ground. Nice, huh? And here you thought that you already knew the names of all of the bastards in that generation of the Bush family!

The actual causes (and there were more than one) of the S&L crisis are still under debate. Many blame the rampant deregulation of the Reagan era. It allowed many S&Ls to get into the same business as banks without the same credentials. In fact, many S&Ls couldn't have even made the grade under the same rigorous regulatory oversight that governed the banks. Deregulation also allowed these S&Ls to become for-profit, make riskier real estate loans, and invest in businesses in which they were not experienced.

Another major cause of the crisis was a practice known in the business as "over-leveraging." Simply put, S&Ls lent far more money than was prudent when interest rates were high in the late 1970s.

★75★
CHARLES KEATING
Millionaire Owner of the "Keating Five"
(1923–)

> "The Senate is a really small club, like the cliché goes. And you really did have one-twentieth of the Senate in one room, called by one guy, who was the biggest crook in the S&L debacle."
> —William Black

There is a special place in Hell reserved for hypocritical bastards like Charles Keating. He swam at the All-American level in college and is now grandfather to five-time Olympic gold medalist Gary Hall, Jr. He was a happily married Arizona businessman and anti-pornography activist during most of the 1950s and 1960s. Today Keating is best known for swindling elderly investors and paying off several U.S. Senators to try and keep out of trouble with federal regulators.

BASTARD AS "ASTERISK"?

Arizona senator John McCain has referred to the "Keating Five" scandal as "my asterisk" and to his attempts to help Keating avoid investigation by federal regulators as the "worst mistake of my life." This of course after Keating made countless campaign contributions to McCain. And after McCain's wife and father-in-law invested over half-a-million dollars in one of Keating's land deals. And after McCain, his wife, and his daughter traveled on Keating's dime no less than nine times, once on his corporate jet! (McCain later paid Keating for the cost of his family's travel.)

The so-called "Keating Five" were five U.S. Senators—Alan Cranston (D–CA), Don Riegle (D–MI), Dennis DeConcini (D–AZ), John Glenn (D–OH), and John McCain (R–AZ)—who were implicated in a scandal involving Keating and his failed Lincoln Savings and Loan Association.

In 1984, Keating took over the Lincoln S&L, hoping to take advantage of recent deregulation. The changing laws would allow his business to invest its depositors' funds in high-risk real estate and speculative junk bonds. In 1985, however, the Federal Home Loan Bank Board (FHLBB) limited the amount of those types of investments to ten percent of the funds on deposit.

Keating fought back when the FHLBB began investigating Lincoln. He commissioned a private study by future Fed Chairman Alan Greenspan who said direct investments were a boon to S&Ls, not a risk. Keating also lobbied the Reagan administration to name his friend Lee H. Henkel, Jr. to the FHLBB in a recess appointment—which does not require Senate confirmation. Henkel resigned shortly after it was revealed that he had several large loans from Lincoln.

The Keating Five met privately with FHLBB Chairman Edwin J. Gray for two hours on April 9, 1987. They tried to pressure Gray to end the investigation of Lincoln. The Lincoln S&L later collapsed and cost U.S. taxpayers over $3 billion.

When news of the scandal broke, the Keating Five were investigated by the Senate Ethics Committee. Cranston received the harshest punishment meted out to the five: a reprimand. Riegle and DeConcini were rebuked for "acting improperly"; Glenn and McCain were criticized for "poor judgment."

Three of the five—Cranston, Riegle, and DeConcini—declined to run for reelection after the scandal. Glenn has since retired. McCain is still in the U.S. Senate; he won the 2008 Republican presidential nomination, but ultimately lost the presidential election to Barack Obama.

And Keating? The *Chicago Tribune* had quite a bit to say about the scandal:

"To say that Charles Keating is a complex man seems a gross understatement. Some see him as an aggressive man who got desperate when the real estate market bottomed out and crossed the line between 'business as usual' and fraud. Others see him as a con artist who finally got caught, a hypocrite who masked his greed with phony piety."

Either way, he got what was coming to him. The legal consequences of his actions included millions in fines and four-and-a-half years in prison. He maintains his innocence to this day. Bastard.

"[John McCain] is a wimp."
—Charles Keating

★76★
LYN NOFZIGER
The Wedtech Wonder
(1924–2006)

> **"I cannot show remorse because I do not believe I am guilty."**
> —Lyn Nofziger

There is no question that President Ronald Reagan was personally honest. It was one of his many admirable qualities. And yet, as the previous chapters have illustrated, he did not always surround himself with people who reflected his own strongly held personal values. Take Franklyn C. "Lyn" Nofziger, for example.

THE QUOTABLE BASTARD

Nofziger was always quotable, especially when it came to discussing former Republican presidents. His most famous zingers include:

1. "I sometimes lie awake at night trying to think of something funny that Richard Nixon said."
2. "[Nixon] and Reagan were not at all alike, because Reagan is an optimist and Dick Nixon wasn't. Yet in some ways they were alike. Neither really liked to talk on the telephone, for instance. And, in a lot of respects, both of them were very much loners."
3. "I'm not a social friend of the Reagans. That's by their choice and by mine. They don't drink enough."

A former newspaper reporter and editor, Nofziger served as Reagan's press secretary while he was governor of California and as one of Nixon's advisors. With

Reagan in the White House in 1981, Nofziger served his old boss as an "advisor" in his new administration.

But Nofziger later left the White House to work as a lobbyist for the defense contractor Wedtech. And that was a problem. By the eighties, the folks at Wedtech were busy bribing public officials to land favorable consideration for Department of Defense contracts. To further complicate matters, Nofziger had steered a multimillion-dollar contract in Wedtech's direction before he left the Reagan White House. Here's the background.

The Wedtech Corporation was founded in the Bronx by a Puerto Rican immigrant named John Mariotta. The baby stroller manufacturer soon became a principal employer in an economically depressed part of New York City.

Mariotta brought in a business partner, Fred Neuberger, who later became majority shareholder. Even so, Wedtech claimed that Mariotta was still the owner; with a Puerto Rican man at the helm, it could continue to take advantage of no-bid Department of Defense contracts that were awarded to minority-owned firms. The company later began paying bribes in the form of company stock to state and federal government officials in order to get the contracts.

When an investigation ensued, numerous Wedtech executives pleaded guilty to bribery and conspiracy charges. They also began rolling on the government officials they had bribed. One of these officials was Mario Biaggi, a former New York City police officer who was first elected to Congress for the Bronx in 1969. He was convicted on fifteen federal felony charges including receiving bribes and obstruction of justice. Former U.S. Attorney General Edwin Meese III was also investigated for receiving bribes from Wedtech.

And then of course there was Nofziger, who was accused of improperly steering a $32 million small-engine contract to Wedtech in return for a job lobbying for the company. Nofziger was charged with violating the Ethics in Government Act which prohibits former government officials from lobbying the government within two years of their departure. Nofziger was convicted, but the verdict was overturned on appeal; the U.S. Supreme Court allowed the appellate court's decision to stand.

Wedtech declared bankruptcy and went out of business in 1987. Nofziger went on to run political campaigns for the likes of Pat Buchanan and Steve Forbes. He never spent a day in jail.

★77★
OLIVER NORTH
Hiding Iran-Contra Behind Fawn Hall's Skirts (and Her Underwear!)
(1943–)

"I thought using the Ayatollah's money to support the Nicaraguan resistance was a neat idea."
—Oliver North

United States Marine Corps Lieutenant Colonel Oliver "Ollie" North graduated from the U.S. Naval Academy and was decorated for his service in Vietnam. President Ronald Reagan named North director for political-military affairs in 1981. Even covered with all those honors, North is seen as the main culprit of the so-called Iran-Contra Affair, though he was never convicted.

The Iran-Contra Affair began after Reagan officials agreed to sell American arms to Iran despite an arms embargo. At first, the weapons sales bought the release of American hostages kidnapped in Lebanon between 1982 and 1992. But weapons were eventually sold for money, too. The Americans then passed these profits on to anticommunist *Contra* rebels fighting Nicaragua's socialist *Sandinista* government.

North was one of the middlemen who brokered the deal, and he came up with the idea of giving the money to the Contras. The Boland Amendment to the 1982 Defense Appropriations Act cut off funding to the rebels, but North went forward with the plan anyway. He used a shell company to send the money to the rebels.

The Lebanese magazine *Ash-Shiraa* first broke the scandal on November 3, 1986. This prompted North and his secretary Fawn Hall to begin editing, destroying, and removing records related to the affair. Reagan publicly fired Hall and North on November 25, 1986.

North invoked the Fifth Amendment before he eventually gave lengthy and televised testimony before Congress in 1987. Nevertheless, he was indicted on twelve charges and convicted of bribery, lying to Congress, and unauthorized destruction of documents. The guilty verdicts were later overturned on appeal because of concerns relating to the use of his immunized Congressional testimony at his trial.

BASTARD GETTING INTO HIS SECRETARY'S PANTIES

In a well-publicized incident, Hall snuck secret government documents out of North's office by hiding them in her boots, under her skirt, even in her underwear. Hall was very attractive, and late night talk show hosts got a lot of mileage out of jokes about how Ollie North had found new ways to get into a woman's pants. Hall was later granted protection from prosecution in exchange for her testimony against North in his 1989 trial. Her official statements included discussion of the underwear in which she had smuggled documents.

Like Watergate burglar G. Gordon Liddy before him, North used the notoriety stemming from his role in the Iran-Contra affair to build cult-hero status among the right wing. Also like Liddy, he cashed in on it. After a failed run as a Republican for a seat representing Virginia in the U.S. Senate, North took to the airwaves. He hosted his own right-wing talk show for several years. He can still be found peddling his skewed notions on politics and patriotism (go figure). He hosts *War Stories with Oliver North* on the Fox News Channel and appears as a frequent "expert commentator" on other shows. He is also the bestselling author of a number of books.

North is also alleged to have been involved in drug trafficking to fund the Contras; he strongly denies these charges. And although a mountain of evidence supports that claim, North has never been charged, and never stood trial for it.

"I would have promised those terrorists a trip to Disneyland if it would have gotten the hostages released. I thank God they were satisfied with the missiles and we didn't have to go to that extreme."

—Oliver North

★78★

JIM WRIGHT
Selling Books Will Lose You Your Congressional Seat
(1922–)

"**Dealmakers [like Jim Wright] are willing to take risks, willing to be tough. They're not coming to Congress anymore.**"
—Tony Coelho, former House Democratic Whip

James Claude Wright, Jr. is a World War II veteran, a career politician, and a former Democratic U.S. Congressman from Texas from 1955 to 1989. He served as House majority leader from 1977 to 1987 and as the fifty-sixth Speaker of the U.S. House of Representatives. He resigned on June 6, 1989.

He was also one of Congress's last dealmakers. In the current age of hyperpartisanship, where no Republican can be brought to cross party lines on a health care reform bill, the days of the dealmakers seem a distant memory. But in the early 1990s, if someone like Wright wanted to get something done, it got done; parties were not as important as the deals that could be made. The loss of such an effective political leader would be a major blow to any ruling political party. The Democrats' loss would be particularly painful.

Wright was forced out of office thanks to what seemed like a very small crime. He avoided paying income tax on the proceeds from *handselling* his books at speaking engagements. Now picture if you will, just how insignificant those proceeds likely were. "Hand sales" are those made directly from an author to a reader; they make up a fraction of total sales numbers for just about any author. Yet Wright was U.S. House Speaker, the third-most powerful person in the country, when he lost his position for precisely that reason. Politicians, lawyers, and popes are adroit at avoiding the costs of their actions, but Wright proved that when important people get nailed for something, it can still be a small-time and well-documented something.

Future Republican House Speaker Newt Gingrich alleged that Wright hand-sold his autobiography, *Reflections of a Public Man*, at his speaking engagements in order to evade Congressional ethics limits on speaking fees. A Congressional committee looked into the claims. There was a substantial paper trail, but no charges were filed, likely because Wright cut a deal.

But Wright wasn't forced to resign because of anything he did. It was because of what he didn't do. While Wright had been a pretty effective majority leader for the better part of a decade, as Speaker he never succeeded in solidifying his position. The wily Gingrich, a bastard of epic proportions in his own right (see his chapter on page 190), capitalized upon Wright's weaknesses. It was just part of Gingrich's long-term strategy to break the Democratic hold on the House, which he accomplished at considerable cost to his soul in the Republican Revolution of 1994.

Wright responded to Gingrich's withering criticisms with nothing more than silence, lost credibility with his party members, and became ineffective as Speaker. And just like that, he was gone.

Wright now teaches at a college in his native Texas, and has written several books, for which he apparently reports any and all payments, from hand sales or otherwise.

★79★

DAN ROSTENKOWSKI
Postage Stamps for Cash as the
Tip of the Graftberg
(1928–)

"I am here in prison for what I admitted to doing tongue-in-cheek."
—Dan Rostenkowski

Daniel "Rosty" Rostenkowski served in the U.S. House of Representatives from 1959 to 1995. He is the son of a Chicago alderman, Joe "Big Joe Rusty" Rostenkowski, and was a product of the infamous Cook County political machine.

A careerist when it came to politics, Rosty's rise began in 1952. At the tender age of twenty-four he won a seat in the Illinois House of Representatives, becoming its youngest member. He was elected to the Illinois State Senate in 1954 and to the U.S. Congress in 1959.

Rostenkowski was a grafter by the time he took his seat in the House. In Chicago politics, no one got ahead without indulging in at least some form of corruption. Rostenkowski's chosen vice was his work as an influence peddler. Beginning in the 1960s, he worked closely with legendary Chicago mayor Richard J. Daley. Rostenkowki ensured that plenty of federally funded pork projects flowed Chicago's way; Daley in turn used this federal patronage to ensure that his political machine remained in power. It was a most profitable relationship for both men.

Rostenkowski's Congressional career spanned nearly four decades. In that time, he became a master at converting his political positions into both monetary and political capital. In the end, he always made sure that his fingerprints were nowhere to be found on the graft that furthered his career. When they finally nailed Rostenkowski, it would be for nickel-and-dime stuff.

In 1981 he became chairman of the powerful House Ways and Means Committee. Here, he had a hand in shaping much of President Ronald Reagan's key legislation, including the Deficit Reduction Act of 1984 and the Tax Reform and Superfund Acts of 1986.

Rostenkowski's political career came to an end in 1994. After a two-year investigation by future U.S. Attorney General Eric Holder, Rostenkowski pleaded guilty to federal mail fraud charges. Holder alleged that Rostenkowski traded postage stamps for cash at the House Post Office. He was also accused of using government money to purchase furniture and ashtrays for friends, and of keeping nonexistent employees on his payroll. Holder's report outlined how Rostenkowski had used these and various other schemes to steal more than $600,000 from the government over a twenty-year period.

Rostenkowski was finished. The scandal forced him to resign his leadership positions; he lost his seat in the 1994 election. He served nearly a year-and-a-half in federal prison before being pardoned by Bill Clinton at the end of his term in 2000.

In their national 1994 campaign, the Republicans led by Newt Gingrich pointed to Rostenkowski as an example of the pervasive corruption they claimed ruled the House under the Democrats. The mid-term elections resulted in a political landslide. The Republican Party assumed control of the House for the first time in decades. In his own way, Rostenkowski added to this.

Rostenkowski's use of graft and patronage to reward and punish made him a creature of another age; he was a vestige of the old-style, wheel-and-deal, big-city machine politics. This older cohort was, as is so often the case in life, unable to adapt to the looming new reality of the more conservative 1990s. Rosty allowed his obsolete methods and mindset to bring down the very party that Roosevelt and Johnson built.

But hey, at least this bastard actually did some jail time.

80

CAROL MOSELEY BRAUN
First Black Female U.S. Senator, Welfare Cheat
(1947–)

> "People just want to hear some common sense ... and I bring to bear the experience in local government and state government and national government—I was the first woman in history on the Senate Finance Committee—not to mention the diplomatic international experience."
> —Carol Moseley Braun

The word "bastard" in its insulting, rather than its more literal sense, is usually reserved for men. After all, there are plenty of other critical, gender-specific terms reserved just for women. Politicians and their particular peccadilloes tend to inspire a unique disgust in the public. The routine, almost casual manner in which they abuse power taints them as "bastards," regardless of their gender. This is especially true of those who steal from a modern-day widows-and-orphans fund like Medicare.

In 1992, the "Year of the Woman," Chicagoan Carol Moseley Braun became the first (and thus far only) African-American woman to be elected to the U.S. Senate. She was born in 1947; her father was a Chicago police officer, and her mother was a medical technician. Moseley Braun attended Chicago public schools, graduated from the University of Chicago Law School in 1972, and became an assistant U.S. attorney. She was elected to the Illinois House of Representatives in 1978, and eventually became assistant majority leader. In 1987, she left the Illinois House to become Cook County Recorder of Deeds.

United States Senator Alan Dixon's decision to vote to confirm Clarence Thomas as a Supreme Court Justice motivated Moseley Braun to challenge Dixon for his seat in 1992. In a major upset, she defeated him in the Democratic primary. Her victory in the 1992 general election was even more surprising in light of longstanding Medicare fraud claims against her.

When their mother passed away in 1989, Moseley Braun and her sister kept an inheritance of nearly $30,000; they should have reimbursed the government for their mother's Medicare-financed nursing home care. This violated federal law, but it was particularly odious in Moseley Braun's case. At the time of her mother's death, she was a well-paid public servant and an experienced attorney capable of earning a good living. She had no reason to cheat the government.

In the end her fraud crippled Moseley Braun's career; she only served one term in the Senate. In 1998, a year when Democrats actually picked up seats in Congress, Moseley Braun was defeated by conservative Republican Peter Fitzgerald. Fitzgerald also served just a single term; in 2004 he lost handily to state Senator and future President Barack Hussein Obama.

BASTARDS ABROAD

In 1996 Moseley Braun went to Nigeria with her fiancé, a Department of Justice-registered agent of that war-torn country. At the time Nigeria was ruled by a brutal strongman named Sani Abacha. He had recently ordered the deaths of dozens of rebels, but Moseley Braun praised this butcher for his "promotion of family values." The unsanctioned trip outraged her chief of staff; he resigned in protest.

After leaving the Senate, Moseley Braun served as U.S. ambassador to New Zealand and ran for president in 2004. She has since founded an organic food company, Good Food Organics. As of this writing she still has not made restitution on the money that her mother's estate owes Medicare.

"All I really want to be is boring. When people talk about me, I'd like them to say, Carol's basically a short Bill Bradley. Or, Carol's kind of like Al Gore in a skirt."
—Carol Moseley Braun

81

BILL CLINTON
The Poobah of Bubbah Politics
(1946–)

"That depends on what the definition of the word 'is' is."
—Bill Clinton

His is the ultimate "rags-to-riches" story. But former Arkansas Governor and U.S. President Bill Clinton's life is also a tale of how a brilliant man's political successes can be nullified by his personal flaws. And like many able politicians, Bill Clinton might be a loveable bastard, but he's a bastard, nonetheless.

━━━━━━━━━━━━ ∽ ━━━━━━━━━━━━

WHAT'S IN A NAME?
Born "William Jefferson Blythe III," our forty-second president never actually knew his biological father. William Jefferson Blythe, Jr. was killed in a car accident three months before his son was born. Billy Blythe was formally adopted by his stepfather Roger Clinton at age fourteen.

While still in high school, Clinton traveled from his home in Arkansas to Washington, D.C., to meet President John F. Kennedy. The experience affected Clinton ever afterward. He emulated Kennedy, entering politics and openly aspiring to the presidency.

Clinton did not limit Kennedy's influence to his personal life. Where JFK had "Fiddle and Faddle," Clinton had what longtime aide Betsey Wright termed "Bimbo Eruptions." Wright served as Clinton's gubernatorial chief of staff for seven years and was his deputy campaign chair in 1992. She coined the phrase "Bimbo Eruptions" to describe the many allegations of the extramarital affairs that surfaced during Clinton's 1992 presidential campaign.

The most publicized of these allegations came from former TV reporter Gennifer Flowers in early 1992. In a tabloid interview Flowers claimed she began a twelve-year-long sexual relationship with then-governor Clinton shortly after first meeting him in 1977. Previously, Flowers had vigorously denied any involvement with Clinton; she'd even threatened a libel suit in 1990 against a radio station that aired similar charges.

Flowers's allegations threatened to derail Clinton's presidential aspirations. When they surfaced, he was polling far behind Massachusetts Senator Paul Tsongas in the race for the New Hampshire primary. To refute them, Clinton and his wife Hillary appeared on a special edition of CBS-TV's *60 Minutes* on January 26, 1992, right after the Super Bowl.

Clinton denied Flowers's allegations but acknowledged his own "wrongdoing" and that his actions were "causing pain in [his] marriage." The interview gave Clinton's campaign a much-needed shot in the arm. He finished a strong second in the New Hampshire primary. He went on to clinch the nomination and the presidency.

Even so, claims of affairs and sexual misconduct continued to dog Clinton all through his presidency. On May 6, 1994, an employee of the Arkansas International Development Commission named Paula Corbin Jones sued Clinton for sexual harassment in federal court. Jones alleged that Clinton pulled her toward him, kissed her neck, and began sliding his hand up the hem of her culottes in his hotel room. She then said Clinton lowered his pants, exposed his penis to her, and said, "Kiss it." Jones said that she feared for her job because she rebuffed Clinton's advances.

During the discovery phase of that case, another set of charges surfaced. This time, Clinton was said to have also had an affair with White House intern Monica Lewinsky. The Jones case was dismissed by U.S. District Judge Susan Webber Wright; the Clintons settled with Jones's legal team for $850,000 when they began to pursue an appeal. Alleged perjury by Clinton during that case led to his impeachment by the U.S. House of Representatives.

The scandal-obsessed press hung breathlessly on descriptions of what Clinton did to his intern Lewinsky with a cigar, an incriminating semen-stained blue dress, and other sordid details of Clinton's personal life. Although his personal popularity took a hit, the Republican-dominated Senate failed to convict him of the charges. He left office more popular than ever with the American public.

"I think what he did in this matter was reprehensible . . . I feel very comfortable with my vote."

—Mark Sanford

★82★
HILLARY CLINTON
"Two for the Price of One"
(1947–)

"I'm not some Tammy Wynette standing by my man."
—Hillary Clinton

Goldwater Girl, top of her class at Wellesley College, corporate lawyer, First Lady, U.S. Senator from New York, and secretary of state. Hillary Clinton has a lot of "firsts" to her credit. Her inclusion in this book is also something of a badge of honor; after all, most bastards are tough and ruthless, and Clinton is both of those things. She is also one of the smartest people to ever enter politics. Plus, let's face it, in order to get ahead as a politician, *and* to stay married to fellow bastard Bill Clinton, you've got to have some bastard in you as well. And Hillary Clinton surely does.

But before she was First Lady or a U.S. Senator or secretary of state, Clinton was a ridiculously successful corporate lawyer. And during that time she became embroiled in the first of what proved to be a number of scandals: a failed 1980s-era real estate deal called Whitewater.

In 1993 Independent Counsel Robert Ray was appointed to investigate the matter. His final report was issued in 2001, the year in which Bill left office, and he cleared the Clintons of all wrongdoing.

The problem for the Clintons: Hillary was anything *but* passive when responding to questions about Whitewater. She was hardly mild-mannered about damned near anything, for that matter. Appointed by Bill to spearhead his health care reform initiative, Hillary came across as high-handed, imperious, and short-tempered in fielding anything other than softball questions from the press.

Whitewater came to be seen by many as "Hillary's Scandal" in large part because several financial documents requested by the Special Counsel's Office mysteriously disappeared from the First Lady's East Wing Office in the White House. They did turn up in a storeroom right down the hall as if by a miracle. It was, of course, the day after a key statute of limitations associated with the ongoing investigation expired. It was all too convenient, especially for the press, which had a field day.

And then a remarkable thing happened: showing herself to be every bit as smart as advertised, Clinton set about reinventing herself. She became a cagier interviewee and someone to be taken seriously on policy matters. When she ran for the U.S. Senate in 2000, she won in a landslide after crossing and re-crossing the state and connecting with voters in ways most of her detractors wouldn't have thought possible.

BASTARD COOKIE RECIPES

Hillary Clinton came into the White House possessed of a pair of sharp elbows. When asked about balancing being a wife and mother with her career as a lawyer, she caustically remarked, "I suppose I could have stayed home and baked cookies and had teas, but what I decided to do was to fulfill my profession which I entered before my husband was in public life." This did not play well with many traditional voters, and the Clintons' popularity took a hit. White House staffers convinced her to attempt to soften her image, giving the kinds of fluff interviews traditionally associated with First Ladyship, and even going so far as to publish her favorite cookie recipes in a women's magazine.

And after eight years of earning a name for herself in the Senate, Clinton emerged as the favorite for the Democratic presidential nomination in the election of 2008. In a bruising primary fight, Clinton took eventual nominee Barack Obama to the wire. She so impressed him that he named her his secretary of state after he won the 2008 election.

Now that is one successful bastard, regardless of gender!

"In the Bible it says they asked Jesus how many times you should forgive, and he said 70 times 7. Well, I want you all to know that I'm keeping a chart."
—Hillary Clinton

★83★
CONGRESS, PART II
The House Banking Scandal
(1775–)

> "Most people think members of Congress—all members of
> Congress—have their hands in the till."
> —Former Indiana Democratic Congressman Lee Hamilton

When it comes to representative government behaving badly, Congress knows how to do it with style. And what the Salary Grab Act was to the nineteenth century, Rubbergate (also known as the House Banking Scandal) was to the twentieth. Both scandals revolved not around the abuse of power so much as the appearance of abuse and the arrogance of those wielding it. Because you've got to be pretty damned conceited to think it's okay to publicly, repeatedly, systematically and with perceived impunity flout rules that govern almost everyone's personal finances. Okay, so it takes more than arrogance. It also takes an ungodly amount of stupidity!

The House Banking Scandal hit the news early in 1992. House Minority Whip Newt Gingrich used the scandal for his own purposes; he pointed to it as an example of "systematic, institutional corruption" that he said was running rampant through the House at the time. Rubbergate was one of the principal scandals that led to seventy-seven Democratic House members being voted out of office in the Republican Revolution of 1994.

It is worth noting that the House Bank was run nothing at all like a normal bank. While computerized systems were the norm for banks in 1992, the House Bank still used paper-and-ink ledgers. Regular statements were not rendered to account holders, nor were they notified when their accounts were overdrawn. Members' deposits were not posted in a timely manner; it could take nearly two months for money to be credited to an account. Further, members of Congress were allowed to overdraw their accounts up to the amount of their next paycheck. The bank *still* never bounced checks written against insufficient funds. It essentially allowed members to overdraw their accounts *ad infinitum*. For this reason, it is inaccurate to say members' nonsufficient funds (NSF) checks were never returned because the bank invariably covered them. The bank also failed to assess fees against members' accounts for the overdrafts.

These loose rules invited abuse. Members of Congress began writing checks they couldn't cash with something resembling absolute freedom from punishment. The worst offender, Democratic Congressman Tommy F. Robinson of Arkansas, wrote 996 NSF checks; his House Bank account was overdrawn for sixteen months. Other members began kiting checks between their House Bank accounts and their personal bank accounts.

The scandal came to public light when the U.S. Government Accountability Office released a report on the House Bank late in 1991. At that point, a group of freshman congressional Republicans demanded an investigation. These men later became known as the "Gang of Seven" or the "Young Turks": Scott Klug (Wis.), Rick Santorum (Pa.), Jim Nussle (Iowa), John Doolittle (Calif.), Frank Riggs (Calif.), Charles Taylor (N.C.), and John Boehner (Ohio).

When the House Ethics Committee conducted an inquiry, Gingrich smelled blood in the water. Many more Democrats than Republicans were implicated; of the top twenty-two check-kiters identified by the committee, nineteen were Democrats. Gingrich then pressured House Speaker Tom Foley to publicly release the names of all members who had written bad checks. Foley, who only wanted to identify the top twenty-two, capitulated and released the entire list. In an early sign of things to come, it was revealed that Gingrich had written twenty bad checks against his own account.

In the end, eleven of the twenty-two worst offenders were defeated in the 1994 election; all but one were Democrats. A later investigation resulted in criminal convictions or guilty pleas for five ex-members, and for the former House Sergeant-at-Arms, Jack Russ.

So there you have it: the United States Congress literally writing checks it can't cash!

KENNETH STARR
The Grand Inquisitor
(1946–)

> "The President inserted a cigar into Ms. Lewinsky's vagina, then
> put the cigar in his mouth and said: 'It tastes good.'"
> —Kenneth Starr

Former U.S. Solicitor-General Kenneth Starr built a long career in both private practice and public service. Unfortunately for the morally upright Texas-born son of a small town minister, he may be best known for spouting a line about cigars and vaginas. And Bill Clinton's impeachment trial, of course. A former judge, Starr abused federal independent counsel law in such a way that he got a sitting president impeached for lying about a private matter.

It's hard to forget the maelstrom Starr released in October 1997. Acting as independent counsel Starr recommended that Clinton be impeached for committing perjury in the Paula Jones case and before the Starr grand jury.

The Republican-dominated House of Representatives held off on a vote until after the November 1998 mid-term elections. Even so, impeachment was a major issue that fall; only about a third of the electorate supported Clinton's demise. In fact, the mid-terms that year defied conventional wisdom. The president's party typically loses big in second-term Congressional elections, but just the opposite happened in 1994. The Republicans lost six seats to the Democrats. House Speaker Newt Gingrich's multiple divorces spoke to his own problems with marital fidelity; he resigned.

Despite the mid-term losses and the lack of popular support, House Republicans pressed forward. On December 19, 1998, Congress approved two Articles of Impeachment against Clinton: perjury before the grand jury and obstruction of justice. Two other articles—abuse of power and perjury in the Jones case—failed to pass. Nevertheless, Clinton became only the second president in U.S. history to face impeachment.

On January 7, 1999, the trial opened in the Senate with U.S. Chief Justice William Rehnquist presiding. Thirteen Republican members of the House Judiciary Committee served as prosecutors during the trial. Among them was the committee chairman, Representative Henry Hyde of Illinois, who dismissed his own four-year-long extramarital affair as a "youthful indiscretion."

Only four witnesses testified at the trial and all did so by videotape: Clinton; Lewinsky; Clinton's friend Vernon Jordan, who got Lewinsky a job working for Revlon Cosmetics at Clinton's request; and Sidney Blumenthal, a senior aide to Clinton.

In the end, the vote fell far short of the two-thirds majority necessary to remove Clinton from office. No Democrats voted to convict on either charge. Ten Republicans voted to acquit for perjury, and five supported release from the obstruction charge. The thirteen House prosecutors paid a heavy price. Only three remained in office after the next round of elections; the rest either lost their individual races or declined to seek reelection.

Even so, Clinton's trial served a longer-term political Republican goal by bringing the "character issue" to the forefront in the next presidential election. Clinton's Vice President Al Gore found himself saddled with much of Clinton's ethical baggage, even though Gore shared none of the blame. Republican presidential nominee George W. Bush ran heavily on this "character," promising to "restore honor and dignity to the White House." And without Clinton's problems with truth under oath, Bush was unlikely to have ever entered the Oval Office as anything other than a visitor.

As for Starr, he currently serves as dean of the Pepperdine University School of Law. He still argues cases in front of the U.S. Supreme Court. He was also a major player in the 2008 grassroots movement to overturn California's gay marriage law.

"Given Kenneth Starr's track record, should we suspect that he's trying to do with innuendo that which he has been unable to do with evidence?"

—Bryant Gumbel

"[Gingrich] told a room full of reporters that he forced the [federal government] shutdown because Clinton had rudely made him and Bob Dole sit at the back of Air Force One . . . Newt had been careless to say such a thing, and now the whole moral tone of the shutdown had been lost. What had been a noble battle for fiscal sanity began to look like the tirade of a spoiled child. The revolution, I can tell you, was never the same."
—Tom DeLay

A Pennsylvania-born military brat, Newt Gingrich earned his PhD in 1971; before entering politics he taught history at the University of West Georgia. He ran for Congress twice before finally winning a seat in 1978. He developed a reputation as a partisan "bomb-thrower." This strategy worked: within eleven years he had become the number-two Republican in the House.

By 1994, Democrats were marred by many recent scandals—from Rostenkowski's stamps to Clinton's affairs; the public wanted something to change. Gingrich tapped into this angst by promoting the "Contract with America" to give his party an edge in the mid-term elections. The contract proposed eight specific reforms the Republicans would enact on the first day of their Congressional mandate if they gained the majority. It worked: the Republicans were swept to power in the House for the first time since 1952.

The Republicans' takeover positioned Gingrich to assume the Speaker's chair at the start of the 104th Congress. But the road was anything but clear. Gingrich and

Clinton would have several bruising legislative battles, culminating in Gingrich's attempt to have Clinton impeached.

Throughout 1995, Gingrich's Congress went to war with the executive branch trying to undo the latter's first-term legislative wins. The mêlée came to a head when the fiscal year ended. Normally, if a federal budget has not been passed by the end of the fiscal year, the government does what it can to keep working. It is customary for the House to pass and for the president to sign various continuing resolutions to keep everything running until the budget is finally approved. Not this time though: Gingrich forced a showdown when he refused to continue talks. The U.S. government ground to a halt and stopped offering all nonessential services for several weeks.

Under pressure from Senate majority leader Bob Dole, who was running for president, Clinton and the Republicans came to an agreement and a budget was passed.

This failed game of chicken stopped the 1994 Republican Revolution dead in its tracks. It also propelled Clinton to reelection in 1996; come 1998, the Republicans would lose precious Congressional seats in the mid-term election. Gingrich later admitted that he shut the government down because he felt slighted over an Air Force One seating arrangement.

SERIAL BASTARD

Gingrich married Jackie Battley, his former high school geometry teacher, in 1962. He later admitted to several affairs before the couple separated in 1980. Gingrich came to Battley's hospital bed while she recovered from uterine cancer surgery. Instead of offering support and comfort, he demanded that she agree to discuss the terms of their upcoming divorce right then and there. He also refused to pay child support to Battley for their two daughters; he forced his ex-wife to rely instead on charitable donations from parishioners at her church. Both Gingrich's second and third wives were women with whom he had affairs while still married to their predecessor.

In 1998 (shortly after his failed attempt to impeach Clinton), Gingrich became embroiled in his own ethical scandal. Gingrich had claimed tax-exempt status for the Progress and Freedom Foundation, an organization he set up to pitch his college course "Renewing American Civilization." Gingrich also admitted to lying to the House Ethics Committee when it was investigating the matter; he was ordered to pay a $300,000 fine. For the first time in U.S. history, the House disciplined a sitting speaker. He resigned as Speaker within a year, two years before his nemesis Clinton left office as one of the most popular presidents of the twentieth century.

"You can't trust anyone with power."

—Newt Gingrich

KATHERINE HARRIS
Lipstick and the Pig
(1957–)

"God is the one who chooses our rulers."
—Katherine Harris

At first blush, former U.S. Congresswoman Katherine Harris seems like too much of a small fry to make the cut of the top 101 bastards in American history. But infamy, like greatness, is all about impact. Through a single dastardly act as Florida Secretary of State in 2000 the otherwise inconsequential Harris cemented her place of dishonor in the Halls of Bastardry.

The hotly contested 2000 election pitted Texas Governor George W. Bush against sitting Vice President Al Gore. It split the country along partisan lines. While outgoing Democratic President Bill Clinton still enjoyed great personal popularity, many voters had grown weary of his scandal-plagued administration. The Republican Party leadership believed that this fatigue, their control of both houses of Congress, and the far-left candidacy of consumer advocate and Green-Party gadfly Ralph Nader would give them an opportunity to win the White House.

On election night, Gore swept most of the Northeast and the Pacific Coast; Bush took the Deep South, the Sunbelt, Mountain West, and Rust-Belt states. Neither side had achieved the 270 electoral votes required to win. And so it all came down to a closely divided Florida. The Sunshine State's election was the responsibility of one woman: one-time corporate vice president and scandal-tinged Republican Florida Secretary of State Harris.

According to exit polls, Florida voters initially favored Gore. As the vote tallies began rolling in, however, things didn't look so clear. At 2:16 A.M. EST, Fox News called the state and the presidency for Bush with only eighty-five percent of the votes counted; Fox's election desk, incidentally, was run by Bush's *cousin* John Ellis. Bush's margin of "victory" in the final count shrank to only 1,784, triggering an automatic recount under Florida election law. The recount further reduced Bush's margin of victory to 327 with one county still outstanding. Gore requested a manual recount in four disputed counties.

Partisan hack Harris announced that she was going to certify the results by the mandated November 15 deadline, well before any hand recounts could have been completed. Gore's camp sued to extend the deadline; the recounts continued.

Harris confirmed Bush as the winner on November 15, but refused to consider the numbers from the recounts then underway. Two days later, the Florida Supreme Court ruled that the hand recount results must be included in the totals; November 26 became the new certification deadline.

SMALL-TIME BASTARD

Before the 2000 election thrust her into the national spotlight, Harris was best known for her involvement with Mitchell Wade. Wade, a military contractor, poured thousands of dollars worth of illegal contributions into Harris's campaign for the state senate. In return Harris requested legislation blatantly favorable to Wade's company.

Harris again declared Bush the winner on November 26, this time by 537 votes. The final decision, though, went to the U.S. Supreme Court. On December 9, all manual recounts terminated pending the court's decision. Three days later, in a highly controversial decision, the U.S. Supreme Court stopped all recounts in Florida, effectively finishing what Harris started and handing the election to Bush.

Harris was rewarded with election to a congressional seat in a safely Republican district; she served two terms before the Republican Party abandoned her when she ran for the Senate in 2006. Eleven people on her staff also resigned shortly after she announced her candidacy, citing her ever more erratic behavior. She got creamed in the general election and is currently out of office.

"People get nervous when they're thrust into the public eye. There was a rumor that someone told Harris that when you're on TV, your makeup washes out so don't be shy with those eyelashes and with that lip color."

—Jay Roach

★87★
MARC RICH
How to Buy a Presidential Pardon
(1934–)

> "Clinton's pardoning of Marc Rich was off the wall."
> —Morley Safer

He was born into a Belgian Jewish family that fled the Nazis and raised him in Brooklyn. Today Marc Rich is an international businessman best known for receiving a suspiciously timed pardon from President Bill Clinton on his last day in office.

Under the U.S. Constitution, the president of the United States has the power of pardons in all federal cases except those of impeachment. This power is absolute, with its roots in the Royal Prerogative of Mercy under English Common Law. The president's decisions regarding whom to pardon and for what are not subject to any review by any court; it is one of the few presidential powers not subject to the system of checks and balances set out in the Constitution. As such it is one of the chief executive's most powerful tools.

Some pardon decisions, of course, have proven controversial. The most famous example is President Gerald Ford's decision to pardon President Richard Nixon after the latter resigned. Similarly, in what was to become known as "Pardongate," Clinton issued 140 pardons and commuted 36 sentences on January 19, 2001, his last full day in office.

Commodities trader Rich received what was probably Clinton's most controversial pardon. Rich became a high profile fugitive after New York U.S. Attorney Rudolph Giuliani indicted him on charges of tax evasion and illegal trading with Iran in 1983. The charges stemmed from accusations that he traded crude oil with Iran during the late 1970s hostage crisis. Rich avoided trial by staying in Switzerland, a country which does not recognize tax evasion as an extraditable offense. An attempt to lure Rich to a country that would hand him over failed. He continued to run a multibillion-dollar business empire from Europe; at one point he was even rated the 242nd richest man in America, though he hadn't lived here in decades.

BASTARD PARDONING . . . BASTARDS?

The more controversial recipients of Clinton's pardons included his half-brother, Roger Clinton. The younger Clinton had served time in prison some ten years earlier on cocaine trafficking charges. Whitewater figure Susan McDougal was also pardoned, having spent more than a year-and-a-half in prison; she had refused to testify before Kenneth Starr's grand jury about Clinton's involvement in Whitewater. Two political allies of Clinton—former Illinois Congressmen Dan Rostenkowski and Mel Reynolds—also received pardons. Reynolds had been convicted of obstruction of justice, bank fraud, and sex crimes including solicitation of child pornography. Clinton reduced his sentence on the sex charges and allowed Reynolds to serve the rest of his time in a halfway house instead of prison.

Rich's pardon raised eyebrows because of his large donations to the Democratic National Committee and to Clinton's presidential library foundation over the years. Clinton justified the pardon on the grounds that charges like those against Rich were typically dealt with in a civil not criminal court. Clinton made Rich agree that he would not use the pardon as a defense to any civil actions that may be brought against him in the United States should he choose to return.

For all that, Clinton was still remarkably tone-deaf on this issue compared to his presidential peers. When the end of his own presidency drew near, George W. Bush did *not* pardon political donors petitioning for relief; he also did very little to protect his own office-holders facing their own looming legal problems. Bush even went so far as rebuffing Vice President Dick Cheney's repeated nagging about a possible pardon for one of his aides. Cheney hoped for a reprieve for his former Chief of Staff Scooter Libby, who was convicted on perjury charges.

As of the time this book was written, Rich has not returned to the United States.

★88★
DICK CHENEY
Torturer-in-Chief
(1941–)

> "9/11 changed everything."
> —Dick Cheney

Longtime politician Dick Cheney has been the secretary of defense, the White House chief of staff, and the U.S. vice president. Cheney has also been a draft-dodger, a liar, a warmonger, and a would-be demolisher of the U.S. Constitution.

To say that the attacks on the World Trade Center and the Pentagon on September 11, 2001 "changed everything" is a gross understatement. 9/11 ushered in a new era of shoeless inspections, pat-down searches, bans of fingernail clippers, and even excessive liquids on flights. But far more worrisome for many Americans were other government responses to foreign terrorism: secret "no-fly lists," extra-judicial detention and interrogation of terror suspects in secret CIA prisons and the U.S. naval base at Guantanamo Bay, Cuba, and stories of the government spying on its own citizens without a warrant. Talk of "enhanced interrogation methods" and "extraordinary renditions" has flooded the news. United States citizens have been held incommunicado on military bases as "unlawful enemy combatants," and a host of other atrocities that most Americans consider abhorrent to their view of the Constitution have occurred in the years since 9/11. All of these factors have helped strain America's relationships with her allies at a time when she can ill-afford to do so.

And all of them can be laid directly at Cheney's doorstep.

As bad as these things are, however, none of them can compare to Cheney's attempted power-grab in the months that followed 9/11. Cheney did not merely try to *circumvent* the system of checks and balances put into the Constitution by the

Founding Fathers. In fact the vice president tried to assume for himself the powers of a dictator; he wanted to be a man accountable to no one and subject to no one's oversight. If he had succeeded, he could have kept whatever secrets he wanted for as long as he damn well pleased.

In 2003 Cheney began refusing to disclose the secrets his office was keeping to the National Archives and Records Administration (NARA). This directly violated an Executive Order issued by former President Bill Clinton in 1995 and reissued by President George W. Bush. The order required all offices within the executive branch to make their papers available to the NARA; it promoted transparency and allowed thorough public oversight of the government's actions.

Cheney refused on the grounds that the orders did not apply to him; he was, after all, both vice president and president of the Senate, which placed him outside of the executive branch. If Cheney had his way, records of his involvement in many Bush administration scandals—from warrantless wiretapping to the administration's involvement, if any, in the Enron debacle—would never see the light of day.

BASTARD TONGUE

Cheney has been notoriously guarded and taciturn during most of his career. But he is also known for making blunt statements that the media loved to convert into sound bites, especially ones like "Reagan proved that deficits don't matter." He even once told Senate Democrat Patrick Leahy of Vermont to "fuck off" right on the Senate floor.

An open government watchdog group eventually sued in federal court to force Cheney's office to turn over its records. United States District Judge Colleen Kollar-Kotelly granted the group's motion. She required Cheney's office to save its records and to turn them over to the NARA in due course. There's no telling what Cheney had already ordered shredded before Kollar-Kotelly's ruling.

When John McCain lost the 2008 election, it was seen in part as a public vote against Cheney. People were fed up with his actions as vice president, his involvement in the Plame/Libby scandal, and his repeated executive branch power grabs. After leaving office the once-hard-to-pin-down Cheney has done a one-eighty. The former vice president has been all over the news, offering harsh criticism of his boss's successor, Barack Obama.

> *"Dick Cheney is one of the most divisive—and disliked—political officials in memory . . . he just presided over the virtual collapse of the American economy and is directly implicated in severe war crimes and other pervasive criminality."*
> —Glenn Greenwald

COLIN POWELL
"Weapons of Mass Destruction" and the Selling of the Iraq War
(1937–)

"There can be no doubt that Saddam Hussein has biological weapons and the capability to rapidly produce more, many more. And he has the ability to dispense these lethal poisons and diseases in ways that can cause massive death and destruction. If biological weapons seem too terrible to contemplate, chemical weapons are equally chilling."
—Colin Powell

Born in New York City to Jamaican immigrant parents, Colin Luther Powell is in many ways the embodiment of the American dream. He was the first African American to be chairman of the Joint Chiefs of Staff, and to serve as both national security advisor and U.S. Secretary of State. A veteran with combat experience in Vietnam, he is also the architect of the Powell Doctrine, a view advocating the need for the use of overwhelming force in war. However, Powell will likely be best remembered by history for selling the need for the invasion of Iraq to the American public and to the United Nations.

After the 9/11 attacks in 2001 the Bush administration set about recasting the Middle East in its preferred image. Invading Afghanistan and defeating Al Qaeda and its Taliban allies was not enough for the Bushies. They wanted another crack at Iraq, so they could "finish the job" that Dubya's "daddy," the first President George Bush, started with the Persian Gulf War in 1991.

How, then, to sell the American public on an invasion of Iraq?

That task fell to U.S. Secretary of State Powell. He had chaired the Joint Chiefs of Staff during Operations Desert Shield and Desert Storm. Powell enjoyed enormous prestige as a result of his tour as chairman of the Joint Chiefs and was nothing if not knowledgeable about the region. Widely seen as a moderating influence in the administration, Powell did not share its hawkish view on Iraq. In fact, he felt that the economic sanctions against Iraq were already working to keep Saddam in check. Still, Bush's team sought support for an invasion and worked to assemble an international coalition to conduct it. So they twisted Powell's arm. Hard.

And on February 5, 2003, speaking before the UN Security Council, Colin L. Powell sold himself out. Relying on intelligence data that was later revealed to be untrustworthy at best and blatantly fabricated at worst, Powell told the UN Security Council:

> *"We know from Iraq's past admissions that it has successfully weaponised not only anthrax, but also other biological agents, including botulinum toxin, aflatoxin, and ricin.*
>
> *But Iraq's research efforts did not stop there. Saddam Hussein has investigated dozens of biological agents causing diseases such as gas gangrene, plague, typhus, tetanus, cholera, camelpox, and hemorrhagic fever, and he also has the wherewithal to develop smallpox."*

All of these claims were false. In its final report, the Iraq Survey Group said that Saddam's chemical, biological, and nuclear weapons programs were destroyed in 1991. In fact, the report said, Saddam was first and foremost concerned with ending the UN sanctions; he maintained those programs as an afterthought.

The speech cost Powell all of his considerable credibility, and it turned out to be for nothing. When the UN Security Council refused to pass such a resolution despite Powell's speech to them, America invaded anyway.

About a year later, White House Chief of Staff Andrew Card asked Powell to resign. Bush replaced him with the more "compliant" Condoleezza Rice.

Powell has since distanced himself from the Bush administration, with mixed results. In 2008 he crossed party lines and endorsed Barack Obama for president;

he continues to advocate on behalf of the troops he once represented as Joint Chiefs chair. However, that does not change the fact that his speech to the UN in 2003 helped put these same troops in harm's way.

"You didn't tell the truth about the war in the Gulf, general!"

—Ron Kovic

★90★
GEORGE W. BUSH
The Rush to Judgment
(1946–)

> "There's an old saying in Tennessee—I know it's in Texas, probably in Tennessee—that says, fool me once, shame on—shame on you. Fool me—you can't get fooled again."
> —George W. Bush

The grandson of a senator, descended from two blue-blooded New England families, and the son of a president, George Walker Bush grew up sucking a Texas-sized silver spoon. Early in life Bush was the picture of the wastrel son of privilege, a failure in business, and initially in politics. During the 1990s Bush used part-ownership of a major league baseball team to pave his way into the governorship of Texas. Less than a decade later, after one of the closest and most bitterly divisive campaigns in American history, he won the presidential election of 2000.

Once in office, Bush set about making radical changes to the U.S. government. He cut taxes several times and relaxed government regulation of everything from environmental protection to lobbying. After the terror attacks of 2001, he and his supporters decided it was time to begin making equally radical changes overseas.

In order to do this, the Bushies reasoned, a rogue nation in the heart of the Arab world needed to be conquered and converted into a showpiece of representative democracy. There seemed no other choice than Iraq, especially since invading that country would be an opportunity to "finish" what Bush's father had started with Operation Desert Storm in 1991.

Team Bush began laying the groundwork for an invasion of Iraq at the beginning of 2002. Over the summer, news reports about Iraq's alleged weapons of mass destruction (WMD) programs kept trickling in. Ultimately, Congress passed the

Authorization for Use of Military Force Against Iraq Resolution of 2002. It cited the WMDs, Saddam's alleged harboring of Al-Qaeda terrorists, as well as his sorry human rights record as justification. The die was cast. Whether or not the UN agreed to go along, America was going to invade Iraq.

Seven years later, the Iraq War has cost the United States billions in treasure and thousands of lives, not to mention over 100,000 Iraqi lives as well. Although he has many sins to answer for, this one is surely the darkest stain on the stunted soul of George Walker Bush.

So why didn't he back out when he had the chance? According to former White House Press Secretary Scott McClellan, Bush was "a leader unable to acknowledge that he got it wrong, and unwilling to grow in office by learning from his mistake—too stubborn to change and grow." McClellan identified several roots of the problem:

- "[Bush]'s fear of appearing weak . . . a more self-confident executive would be willing to acknowledge failure."
- "The personal pain he would have suffered if he'd had to acknowledge that the war against Saddam may have been unnecessary. . . . [He] was not one to look back once a decision was made. Rather than suffer any sense of guilt and anguish, Bush chose not to go down the road of self-doubt or take on the difficult task of honest evaluation and reassessment."
- "[A]nother motive for Bush to avoid acknowledging mistakes was his determination to win the political game at virtually any cost."
- "Bush's insistence on remaining true to his base. . . . As far as Bush and his advisers (especially Karl Rove) were concerned, being open and forthright in such circumstances was a recipe for trouble."

"You start to pity [Bush] until you remember how vast the wreckage is. It stretches from the Middle East to Wall Street to Main Street and even into the heavens, which have been a safe haven for toxins under his passive stewardship. The discrepancy between the grandeur of the failure and the stature of the man is a puzzlement. We are still trying to compute it."

—Frank Rich

★91★

JOHN YOO
A Torquemada for All Americans
(1967–)

"Congress's definition of torture . . . the infliction of severe mental or physical pain—leaves room for interrogation methods that go beyond polite conversation."

—John Yoo

"A lawyer in the Department of Justice's Office of Legal Counsel (OLC), Korean-born and Pennsylvania-raised John Choon Yoo was the principal author of the Bybee Memos. More formally known as the Interrogation Opinion, the collection of letters to the CIA was named for their signatory, Bush administration lawyer and now U.S. Court of Appeals Judge Jay Bybee.

Yoo wrote them in response to a CIA request for advice on how far interrogators could legally go in their questioning of terrorism suspects. What he wrote was a fifty page memo that claimed to define "torture," under both United States and international law:

> "Acts inflicting, and that are specifically intended to inflict, severe pain or suffering, whether mental or physical . . . [w]e further conclude that certain acts may be cruel, inhuman, or degrading, but still not produce pain and suffering of the requisite intensity to [constitute torture].

> Physical pain amounting to torture must be equivalent in intensity to the pain accompanying serious physical injury, such as organ failure, impairment of bodily function, or even death. For purely mental pain or suffering to amount to torture . . . it must result in significant psychological harm of significant duration, e.g., lasting for months or even years. We conclude that mental harm also must result from one of the predicate

acts listed in the statute, namely: threats of imminent death; threats of infliction of the kinds of pain that would amount to physical torture; infliction of such physical pain as a means of psychological torture; use of drugs or other procedures designed to deeply disrupt the senses, or fundamentally alter an individual's personality; or threatening to do any of these things to a third party . . . . We conclude that the statute, taken as a whole, makes plain that it prohibits only extreme acts."

In a later Bybee memo, the OLC expressed its opinion on ten techniques to be used to question "high value detainee" Abu Zubaydah as part of an "increased pressure phase." These techniques included face slapping; slamming against a wall; sleep deprivation for up to seventy-two hours; stress positions designed to cause muscle fatigue; confinement in a dark box with insects; and waterboarding. The memo concluded that none of the techniques constituted torture.

The memos prompted an investigation by the Justice Department's Professional Responsibility division into whether they could be considered competent legal advice. Many believe they only served to enable the administration to cover itself for actions it had already decided to take. Further, the memos could prove problematic for their authors when they travel abroad. Spain has already launched a war crimes investigation against those involved; it is expected to ask the United States for their extradition.

Yeah. Good luck with that.

As for John Yoo, where the terror memos don't seem to have hurt his former boss's career, his enthusiastic embrace of the legal "rebranding" of the notion of "torture" put a capper on his own career path in the Justice Department. He resigned in disgust at his being passed over repeatedly for promotion, and went back to teaching law.

He continues to argue for the legality of "enhanced interrogation techniques."

"This is the scum whose enthusiasm for torture and zeal for unfettered executive power is so extreme, he once responded to the theoretical question 'If the president deems that he's got to torture somebody, including by crushing the testicles of the person's child, there is no law that can stop him?' with 'I think it depends on why the President thinks he needs to do that.'"

—Lilian Segura

★92★
KEN LAY AND ENRON
"Business Ethics" for the New Millennium
(1942–2006)

> "We treat others as we would like to be treated ourselves. We do not tolerate abusive or disrespectful treatment. Ruthlessness, callousness, and arrogance don't belong here."
> —Enron Corporation Code of Ethics, 2000

We've established that a group of people can be "bastards" collectively, so why not a corporation? Well, if ever there was a "bastard corporate entity," it was Texan energy giant Enron.

By the year 2000 the name "Enron" became synonymous with fraud and corruption. The company's dramatic rise and stunning fall exposed major faults in America's regulation of the energy and financial services industries.

Enron was founded in the mid-1980s as a power transmission and natural gas company. It later branched out into energy futures and online commodities trading. The company's high stock price and innovative trading methods won it accolades; *Forbes* dubbed it "America's Most Innovative Company" from 1996 to 2001.

At one point there were even rumors that Enron chairman Ken Lay would be named as energy secretary if his personal friend George W. Bush won the 2000 presidential election. With its stock soaring and the right friends in the right places, there seemed to be no limit on how high the company could fly.

Too bad it was all an illusion.

The truth is that Enron really never made a dime. It lost hundreds of millions of dollars year in, year out, and it shielded those losses from disclosure with various corporate entities and all manner of what many accountants call Cleverly Rigged Accounting Ploys (use your imagination to figure out that acronym!).

Enron's accounting company Arthur Andersen abdicated its role of watchdog. In fact, the firm actively enabled Enron's fraud by allowing it to utilize market to market accounting. Enron was then able to book the future value of an as-yet unfinished deal as current revenue.

Enron bought real power plants with its artificial money. It then sold the power on the open market for what the market would bear. To this end, it orchestrated power plant shutdowns during periods of high demand, like the summer of 2000 in California. This price manipulation drove California's largest utility, Pacific Gas & Electric (PG&E), into bankruptcy. PG&E had to be bailed out by California's taxpayers to regain its solvency.

When Enron finally went bankrupt, tape recordings of phone calls between the company's traders were made public. In numerous profanity-laced conversations, Enron's traders openly bragged about driving energy prices so high that elderly people could not afford to pay their electric bills.

BASTARDS ACTUALLY BROUGHT TO JUSTICE!

Enron's CEO, Jeffrey Skilling (who left the company right before the collapse), was convicted on multiple fraud, conspiracy, and insider trading counts. He was later sentenced to twenty-five years in prison, but that sentence was recently overturned on appeal. The company CFO Andrew Fastow turned state's evidence and received a six-year term. He is presently incarcerated at a minimum security federal prison camp that is, ironically, adjacent to the federal "supermax" prison in Florence, Colorado. And it couldn't happen to a nicer bunch of guys.

Enron's fake dealings had very real-world consequences for many innocent people. Its employees' retirement fund contributions were not matched with cash but with shares of Enron stock. When the company went under, its employees' nest eggs did too.

After it all came crashing down, Enron Chairman Ken Lay was convicted on ten counts of fraud. He was facing over 175 years in prison, but died of a timely heart attack prior to his sentencing.

So this is a case where one of the principal "bastards" in question actually died before he could begin serving his richly deserved life sentence, and the other has been serving a lengthy jail term in prison!

Now *that* is justice!

★93★

DAVID VITTER
Sometimes a Senator Just Needs a Diaper
(1961–)

"We do not need international help to stop corruption, we need strong Louisiana Leadership."
—David Vitter

Louisiana born and bred, David Vitter is also a product of Harvard and a Rhodes Scholar. Unlike fellow Southern politician bastard Bill Clinton, Vitter actually finished his course of study at Oxford University; obviously the guy is one smart cookie. And like his Louisiana Senate predecessor and fellow bastard Huey Long, Vitter has demonstrated himself to be both an opportunist and a "reformer."

And he likes hookers. A lot.

Vitter rose from the Louisiana state legislature to the U.S. House and Senate on the strength of his solid conservative values. He has fought against abortion rights and for gun rights. He opposes expansion of gambling, called for the repeal of the estate tax, and has worked tirelessly to increase government military spending.

First elected to Congress in 1999 in a special election after House Speaker Bob Livingston's resignation in an adultery scandal, Vitter has always been quick to point out the moral shortcomings of others. Apparently in his frequent readings of the Bible he missed that whole "Let he who is without sin cast the first stone" thing. After winning reelection handily in a safe Republican district, Vitter won a Senate seat in 2004.

Allegations that Vitter had repeatedly cheated on his wife with prostitutes began to swirl around him in 2002; they forced him to withdraw from the Louisiana governor's race. These rumors resurfaced in 2007 when the "D.C. Madam" scandal involving Deborah Jeane Palfrey hit the news. Vitter's phone number appeared in records seized by federal agents in connection with the investigation; Vitter acknowledged being Palfrey's customer.

And yet the first time through the list, the Feds actually missed Vitter's number. So who does the public have to thank for catching this sanctimonious bastard in the act?

Hustler publisher, free speech advocate, and all-around vindictive son-of-a-bitch Larry Flynt. Flynt paid private detectives to comb through the reams and reams of phone numbers in Palfrey's records looking for someone exactly like Vitter. In a fitting irony, if Vitter owes both his Congressional career and his ongoing problems with his infidelity to anyone aside from himself, it's Flynt.

Flynt was also the person behind the revelations that Livingston was having an affair back in 1999. He had done much the same thing in Livingston's case as he had in Vitter's; the only difference seemed to be that he paid operatives to cull through the phone records of a Louisiana cat-house instead of those of a D.C. madam.

BABY BASTARD

Vitter paid prostitutes up to $300 to diaper him, among other things. Apparently all that moralizing during his day gig makes him want to go back to a "simpler time" in his life?

Once exposed Vitter copped to his "sin" in the requisite news conference where he asked for forgiveness from everyone, including, of course, his wife. She stood stoically behind him, as have so many other wronged women in the history of modern political sex scandals. Newspapers back in New Orleans began to report that he had once been a client of a since-shut-down New Orleans brothel. Vitter emphatically denies this, but the ex-madam who ran the place insists he did use her services, even recalling him as a nice guy: "Just because people visit a whorehouse doesn't make them a bad person," she's been quoted as saying. Yeah, and just because someone's a U.S. Senator doesn't make them a good one, either!

> *"Mr. Vitter is a holier-than-thou family-values panderer. He recruited his preteen children for speaking roles in his campaign ads and, terrorism notwithstanding, declared that there is no 'more important' issue facing America than altering the Constitution to defend marriage."*
>
> —Frank Rich

94

SCOOTER LIBBY
When Lying Really Does Have Consequences
(1950–)

> "[Libby] is intensely partisan . . . in that if he is your counsel, he'll embrace your case and try to figure a way out of whatever noose you are ensnared in."
> —Jackson Hogan

Irv Lewis "Scooter" Libby graduated from all the right schools, including Yale Law School, and at one time had a distinguished career both in and out of government as one smart lawyer. His involvement in the George W. Bush administration scandal "Plamegate" has cost him both his reputation and his license to practice law. It likely should have cost him more.

Libby has held positions under several Republican presidents. He first joined the U.S. State Department's policy planning staff in 1981 and later served in the Bureau of East Asian and Pacific Affairs. During the first Bush administration, he served as under-secretary of defense for policy. In 2001, he became Vice President Dick Cheney's chief of staff. A dedicated neoconservative, Libby was one of the signatories to the Project for the New American Century's 2000 report that called for increased defense spending.

He was also the only Bush Administration official indicted and convicted in the Plamegate scandal for exposing the identity of CIA counter-proliferations operative Valerie Plame Wilson.

Libby was one of several sources who leaked Plame's status as a covert agent to reporters including conservative columnist Bob Novak of the *Chicago Tribune* and Judith Miller of the *New York Times*. Unlike fellow Bushie Karl Rove and Assistant Secretary of State Richard Armitage though, Libby lied under oath when questioned about Plamegate by federal prosecutors. Convinced of Libby's perjury, U.S. Attorney and Plamegate Special Counsel Patrick Fitzgerald indicted Libby on several counts of obstruction of justice, perjury, and lying under oath to federal investigators.

This effectively ended Libby's career in public service. He resigned when he was indicted in connection with the scandal. Through the trial, it became clear that Armitage, not Libby, was the primary leaker; Libby only passed Armitage's information along to Novak. Even so, Libby was convicted on charges of perjury, obstruction of justice, and lying to investigators.

WHAT'S IN A NAME?

No one has ever seemed to be able to get a straight answer from Libby about his first name, or, for that matter, about his nickname "Scooter." Ostensibly named after his father, Connecticut banker Irving Lewis Leibowitz, Libby has gone by "Scooter" for most of his life. According to *New York Times* reporter Eric Schmitt, Libby's elder brother says that "'I' stands for Irv. His nickname 'Scooter' derives from the day Mr. Libby's father watched him crawling in his crib and joked, 'He's a Scooter!'" At some point Libby also changed his family name from Leibowitz to the more WASP-y "Libby."

Throughout his trial, Libby had requested reams upon reams of classified information and documents. Libby's requests raised suspicion that he may have been employing "graymail"—the threat of revealing national secrets—as part of his defense. The fact that Bush commuted his thirty-month prison sentence only strengthened these rumors.

To Bush's credit, he allowed Libby's conviction to stand, even though he voided the jail term portion of it. Effectively disbarred, Libby has since found it difficult to do the sort of work he did while a member of the D.C. bar. This cost Bush plenty of headaches during his remaining months in office. His vice president (and Libby's former boss) Dick Cheney relentlessly lobbied the president to pardon Libby until their last day in office. Bush adamantly refused to do so.

But hey, at least the little bastard didn't have to actually spend a day in jail.

95

ALBERTO GONZALES
Attorney General as Consigliore, Part II
(1955–)

> "I don't recall."
>
> —Alberto Gonzales sixty-four times during Senate testimony

If ever there was a political hack that got by on his friendships, it's George W. Bush administration's Attorney General Alberto Gonzales. Involved up to his eyeballs in all of the shady goings-on in the Bush White House, the former Texas state Supreme Court judge and White House Counsel is probably best remembered for being at the heart of the spate of politically motivated firings known as "Attorneygate."

One of the Attorneygate lawyers was John McKay, U.S. Attorney for the Western District of Washington in Seattle. McKay had been a stalwart Republican and loyal to Bush before his dismissal. He had handled the prosecution of the alleged "Millennium Bomber" Ahmed Ressam to great acclaim. There was even talk of a possible nomination to the federal bench.

All that changed when McKay refused to call a grand jury to look into claims of voter fraud connected to Washington's hotly contested 2004 gubernatorial election. Democrat Christine Gregoire had beaten Republican Dino Rossi and won the state by a few hundred votes; the state Republican Party had blown through its court appeals trying to get the results reversed. Bush couldn't seem to do any better with someone loyal to his cause. The "lawyer" nominated to replace McKay was former Congressman Rick White, an evangelical Christian and member of the 1994 "Freshman Class" of House Republicans. The nomination didn't go far. The *Seattle Times* later reported that White had let his law license lapse and was thus not even authorized to practice law in Washington!

Other fired U.S. attorneys had wound up on the "wrong side" of high-profile prosecutions of Republicans. One of them was Carol Lam, the U.S. Attorney for the Southern District of California; she convicted Republican Congressman Randy "Duke" Cunningham of fraud and bribery.

During the investigation that followed Gonzales said it was an "overblown personnel matter." A Department of Justice Inspector General's report, however, blasted Gonzales and other higher-ups. The report said, "The Department's removal of the U.S. attorneys and the controversy it created severely damaged the credibility of the Department and raised doubts about the integrity of Department [prosecution] decisions." The report further noted that the Bush administration would not hand over any documents for which the inspector general called. Administration officials believed to be involved in the firings—Karl Rove, Harriet Miers, and others—refused to cooperate with the investigation. Gonzales resigned shortly after the report came out; eight other senior officials at the DOJ followed him.

WHAT'S IN A WORD?

During "Attorneygate," seven U.S. attorneys were fired on December 7, 2006, midway through Bush's second term. The cuts were allegedly made for political reasons. While U.S. attorneys are political appointees and serve at the pleasure of the president, a mass firing midway through a president's term was unheard of. Many viewed the dismissals as proof positive of the political nature of the Justice Department under Gonzales.

As of early 2010, Gonzales has been unable to secure employment as a lawyer; his struggle is completely unprecedented for a former U.S. Attorney General. He is currently working as a diversity recruiter at Texas Tech University.

> *"Nobody is surprised to learn that the Justice Department was lying when it claimed that recently fired federal prosecutors were dismissed for poor performance. Nor is anyone surprised to learn that White House political operatives were pulling the strings. What is surprising is how fast the truth is emerging about what Alberto Gonzales, the attorney general, dismissed just five days ago as an 'overblown personnel matter.'"*

—Paul Krugman

96

ELIOT SPITZER
Hookergate
(1959–)

> "I'm a fucking steamroller and I'll roll over you or anybody else."
> —New York Governor Eliot Spitzer to New York State Assembly Minority Leader
> James Tedisco

The Bronx-born son of an overachieving real estate titan, Eliot Spitzer had great expectations placed on him from an early age. He was tough-talking and hard-driving, a Princeton-educated yuppie who graduated high in his class at Harvard Law School. Spitzer always seemed to know exactly what he was doing and exactly to whom he was doing it.

After a brief turn in private practice, Spitzer worked for the legendary Robert Morgenthau in the Manhattan District Attorney's office. While an assistant DA, Spitzer pursued organized crime's involvement in Manhattan's garment industry with an innovative application of antitrust laws. He was instrumental in bringing down the Gambino crime family; he went after the trucking industry monopolies that brought them the lion's share of their ill-gotten gains. Spitzer also prosecuted other kinds of racketeering including prostitution rings which, as we shall see later, came back to haunt him.

After another stint in private practice Spitzer ran as a Democrat for New York State Attorney General in 1998. He won a close race over Republican incumbent Dennis Faso.

Campaigning on his successes as attorney general, Spitzer was elected to New York's governorship in 2006. The beginning of his term in office was promising; Spitzer had always been someone who knew how to get things done. He promised to balance the state budget and was initially successful. But within a year the state was once again running a deficit, and Spitzer was openly feuding with members of his own party in the legislature over his high-handedness and their well-known stubbornness.

And all this time Elliot Spitzer had a dark secret. He had a thing for high-priced hookers. On several occasions over the course of a decade—all while serving as attorney general and then as governor—Spitzer went to Washington, D.C., to patronize high-priced call girls from the "Emperors Club VIP Service"; he spent upwards of $80,000 on them. Spitzer resigned the governorship when it was revealed that he was Emperors Club's Client No. 9.

BASTARD CRIMEFIGHTER

When he became New York's Attorney General, Spitzer used the office to pursue a different kind of organized crime: The rampant fraud and corruption taking place on Wall Street. In one of his cases, Spitzer successfully prosecuted Merrill Lynch tech stock analyst Henry Blodget. Blodget became famous for predicting that Amazon.com's stock would rise to over $400 a share. His career in the industry was short-lived, however, when the truth came out. Blodgett was issuing "buy" and "strong buy" recommendations on stocks that he was disparaging in internal e-mails as "piece[s] of shit." He was prosecuted for fraud, first by Spitzer and then by the Securities and Exchange Commission, and was ultimately banned from the industry for life. Spitzer also prosecuted a number of cases involving the collapse of Enron.

The writer F. Scott Fitzgerald once remarked that there are "no second acts in American lives." Don't try to tell Spitzer that. After tossing his career in the dumpster over the call-girl scandal, Spitzer is busy working on rebuilding his reputation in anticipation of some sort of "second act."

"If you're a frugal governor who doesn't even like paying his political consultant bills, as opposed to an Arab sheik or a Vegas high roller, do you really need to shell out $4,300, plus minibar expenses, to a shell company for two hours with a shady lady? Aren't there cheaper hooker hook-ups on Craigslist? It makes you wonder how sharp Eliot Spitzer's pencil was on the state's fiscal discipline."

—Maureen Dowd

★97★

TOM DELAY
The "Hammer" Gets Nailed
(1947–)

"I *am* the federal government."
—Tom DeLay, to the owner of Ruth's Chris Steak House, after being told to
put out his cigar because of federal government regulations banning smoking
in the building

Elected to Congress in 1984, Tom DeLay is a born-again Christian who has backed pro-life and anti-evolution causes all the way through his career. He has also fought for pro-business causes; he has supported a bid to repeal the ban on ozone-depleting chlorofluorocarbons and other laws he deemed unduly taxing to business. In the late 1980s, he made a name for himself as one of the main critics of the National Endowment for the Arts, calling for it to be defunded.

IT'S ALL IN THE NICKNAME

"The Hammer" has been known by a number of nicknames over the course of his political career. Before he first ran for public office he owned his own pest control service; once he was elected to the Texas House of Representatives in 1978, he became known (not surprisingly) as "the Exterminator." Within a year his hard-partying ways earned him the sobriquet "Hot-Tub Tom."

DeLay didn't truly gain a prominent place in national politics until 1994. It was then, as House Majority Whip, he acquired the nickname "The Hammer" for his unwavering ability to enforce party control and to exact vengeance on his rivals in both parties.

One of his favorite tactics was to threaten to "primary"—to fund and endorse a primary election challenger—any congressman who voted against a bill he was trying to pass. One of these key votes was the impeachment of U.S. President Bill Clinton. DeLay refused to allow a compromise option during the trial, even though a vote of censure was favored by moderates in both parties.

DeLay did not always see eye to eye with the rest of the Republican leadership. He felt that Newt Gingrich was not sufficiently committed to Christian values. DeLay even tried to stage a coup to depose Gingrich from the speakership in 1997.

Still, DeLay was elected House majority leader in 2003. During this time, he backed a bid to gerrymander Texas's Congressional districts to assure a "permanent Republican majority." Democratic members of Texas's legislature fought back by leaving the state to prevent a vote on the proposal. He was also involved in the "K Street Project," an effort to sway key lobbying firms to hire Republican activists.

DeLay was forced from office in 2005 when he was indicted on multiple federal and state charges. He was accused of money laundering and violation of campaign finance laws, among other things. He resigned as majority leader upon his indictment and declined to seek reelection in 2006.

In 2009 the "Hammer" appeared on TV's *Dancing with the Stars*. Before leaving the competition citing back problems, DeLay pranced around on stage in a glittering red-white-and-blue sequined American flag costume that would have made Liberace blush.

As for the charges against him, the prosecutor who first brought them has demonstrated a good deal of resolve: "There are particular cases pending that are enormously important to this state, this country, and democracy itself. If they are not resolved during the forthcoming last year of my term I will offer my assistance on those matters on a pro bono basis to my successor."

"Guns have little or nothing to do with juvenile violence. The causes of youth violence are working parents who put their kids into daycare, the teaching of evolution in the schools, and working mothers who take birth control pills."
—**Tom DeLay, on the causes of the Columbine High School massacre**

★98★
KARL ROVE
"Just Get Me a Fucking Faith-Based Thing. Got It?"
(1950–)

> "You can fool some of the people all of the time, and those are the people we should concentrate on."
>
> —Karl Rove

While many political figures in the history of the United States have earned the nickname of "bastard," few have worked harder and longer to earn it by dint of petty, mendacious action after petty, mendacious action than former Bush staffer Karl Christian Rove. Rove was born in Denver, raised in Nevada, and went to high school in Salt Lake City. There, he won student council elections despite being "scrawny" and "uncool."

Rove's first brush with national attention came during his quest for the chairmanship of the College Republican National Committee. During the group's 1973 convention, tapes of Rove teaching underhanded tactics (like rooting through opponents' garbage cans) were leaked to the *Washington Post*. This drew an FBI probe, but Rove's campaign manager (future Reagan and Bush political aide) Lee Atwater swore in an affidavit that the tapes reflected coffee-break conversation in jest. The FBI closed its investigation and Rove became chair of the College Republicans.

Atwater mentored Rove and taught him that "bare knuckles" weren't ever enough. Atwater was known for wanting "to always drive one more stake" into a political opponent. In Rove, Atwater found an apt pupil; Rove would one day use the bastard playbook to surpass his erstwhile mentor.

Rove met the Bush family when then-Republican National Committee Chairman George H. W. Bush secured Rove a full-time job with the Republican Party. He has remained close to the family ever since, advising George W. ("Dubya") Bush's failed

1978 Congressional campaign and George H. W. ("Poppy") Bush's abortive 1979 presidential campaign.

Rove's arsenal of dirty tricks also includes push polls. While working on the younger Bush's 1994 campaign for the Texas governorship, Rove asked voters pointed questions: would they vote for incumbent Texas Governor Ann Richards if they knew most of her staffers were lesbians? He got the answers he wanted and started plenty of trouble for the opposing camp.

BUGGY BASTARD

Throughout the 1980s, Rove pioneered direct mail political fundraising, offering his services to hundreds of Republican candidates. In 1986, while working on William Clements, Jr.'s Texas gubernatorial campaign, Rove alleged that Democrats had planted listening devices in his office. In fact, Rove bugged his own office to make his opponent look bad and to attract votes.

Such rumor-mongering has become a Rove staple. In 2000, when Bush Jr. was running for president, Rove derailed a primary challenge by Arizona Senator John McCain by spreading rumors in Southern states that the senator had fathered an illegitimate child with a black woman. In the 2004 presidential election, Rove was said to have been in league with the group Swift Boat Veterans for Truth who smeared Senator John Kerry's Vietnam service record. He also made sure the Homeland Security terror alert threat level rose whenever Kerry advanced in the polls.

During Dubya's second term, Rove found himself embroiled in several of the administration's many scandals. He was one of two sources who leaked the identity of CIA operative Valerie Plame to reporter Robert Novak who outted her in his column. He also was a central figure in the Attorneygate scandal when several U.S. attorneys deemed disloyal to Bush were hastily fired. Rove selected the White House's candidates for dismissal, though the Justice Department did the firing.

After the 2006 Congressional elections returned the Democrats to power, Rove resigned "to spend more time with his family"; in truth he was given the boot. Even the thick-headed Dubya by now saw him as a liability.

He has yet to be indicted for any wrongdoing. Since his resignation Rove has popped up on (go figure) Fox News Channel as a political commentator.

SARAH PALIN
'Nuff Said!
(1964–)

> "I think on a national level your Department of Law there in the White House would look at some of the things that we've been charged with and automatically throw them out."
> —Sarah Palin

There's plenty to say about Sarah Palin. Her political career and time as governor of Alaska, her historic run for the vice presidency in 2008, her son's problems with drug abuse and petty crime, her daughter's unwed teen pregnancy, her tax problems, and the investigation into her mishandling the firing of her chief law enforcement official due to a conflict of interest have all been noted in the media and the annals of history. We're going to focus on just two small aspects of her checkered career: her at times hilarious inability to keep the facts straight, and her willful misuse of the phrase "fiscal conservative."

In September of 2008, Palin accepted Arizona Senator John McCain's offer to join him on the Republican ticket; in her speech accepting that nomination, she polished her credentials as a "fiscal conservative" and energized the Republican Party's conservative base. Too bad it was mostly fantasy. This should surprise no one who has learned anything about Palin. In fact, it confirms two things about Ol' Snowmobile Sarah. First, Caribou Barbie might not know much, but what she knows, she knows down to her manicured toenails. Second, she doesn't lack for guts.

As for Palin's solid record of "fiscal conservatism" (two words that rank right up there with "pro-life" and "gun-rights" in the hearts of the denizens of the American right wing), there is room for debate about whether or not she even understands the term.

In speech after speech, both before she helped McCain lose the 2008 election and afterward, Palin has alternated between savaging the media covering her and claiming that she's a fiscal conservative. This includes her famously ludicrous claim to have said, "thanks, but no thanks" to the Feds when they tried to force her to take the $300 million to pay for that much-needed "Bridge to Nowhere." The truth is that she did take the money, she just didn't build the bridge!

So since when is Palin a fiscal conservative?

Since she was mayor of Wasilla, Alaska? If Palin was so fiscally conservative during her tenure as mayor of Wasilla, why did she raise the sales tax (even on food) to a crushing rate? While it's true that she cut corporate taxes to the bone, people in Wasilla saw their individual tax rates skyrocket during her time in office there. Why did she leave the city $6 million in debt? Was the municipal debt level that high when she took office during the late 1990s? Nope. It was at zero.

Okay, so maybe Palin became a fiscal conservative after she became governor in 2006.

If that's the case, then why did she borrow money from the state to pay for necessities such as road maintenance (those roads she couldn't get the Feds to pay for, that is)? The state was enjoying record surpluses in revenue before oil prices crashed in late 2008! Since when is handing out legally collected state revenues as "cash dividends" to Alaskan voters while borrowing money to fix the roads "sound, conservative fiscal policy"?

BASTARD DIVA

"She is a diva. She takes no advice from anyone. She does not have any relationships of trust with any of us, her family or anyone else. Also, she is playing for her own future and sees herself as the next leader of the party. Remember: Divas trust only unto themselves, as they see themselves as the beginning and end of all wisdom."—An anonymous McCain adviser complaining to CNN about Palin going off-script

Palin announced her resignation from office effective in August 2009. Maybe she's got her sights set on a presidential run of her own in 2012? To paraphrase one of her own speeches, how do ya see that workin' out fer ya?

"Wasilla hillbillies looting Neiman Marcus from coast to coast."
—An angry McCain aide describing Palin's $150,000 shopping spree

★100★
MARK SANFORD
The Wages of Hypocrisy
(1960–)

"I think it would be much better for the country and for (President Clinton) personally (to resign)... I come from the business side.... If you had a chairman or president in the business world facing these allegations, he'd be gone."
—Mark Sanford

Republican real estate developer Mark Sanford first held office when he was elected to Congress in 1994 at age thirty-four. He became famous for drawing the line on President Bill Clinton's behavior in connection with his affair with staffer Monica Lewinsky during the president's impeachment trial during the late 1990s. When asked during a December 1998 interview why he thought Clinton was able to survive attempts to remove him from office after the Lewinsky scandal, Sanford said: "In politics you can get away with anything as long as it's what's expected .... If people expect you to be a rascal, you can be a rascal."

Sanford traded on his integrity and his reputation as a devoted family man with a terrific marriage as part of the package when he began his political career; he served three terms in Congress and made a successful run for South Carolina governor in 2002. During that time he developed a contentious relationship with South Carolina's Republican-controlled legislature.

His stature with conservatives jumped considerably when he threatened to refuse all or part of President Barack Obama's proposed stimulus money, intended to restart the stalled economy in early 2009. At this point Mark Sanford's world began to fall apart.

Turns out that Sanford had been conducting a secret affair for many years with an Argentine commodities broker, María Belén Chapur. Honest Mark Sanford, whose reputation was built on integrity, had lied about this affair repeatedly. Sanford, the same upstanding man who loosed the pigs on legislators he felt were misusing public money by supporting pork projects, had himself misused public funds. In Sanford's case he used them to organize several trade missions to South America to see his mistress; something he'd been doing at least since 2004.

It all came to a head over Father's Day weekend of 2009, when devoted family man Sanford disappeared. He told his aides that he was going to spend a few days hiking the Appalachian Trail. So what did Sanford really do? On June 18 he went to Argentina. And from then until June 24, no one had any idea where he was.

Sanford was finally spotted by a journalist as he stepped off a plane in Atlanta. Speculation mounted as to what he had been doing and where he had been doing it while supposedly hiking the Appalachian Trail. And that was when Sanford broke his silence and began to talk. And talk. And talk.

BASTARD ULTIMATUM

Sanford's wife Jenny knew about his on-again-off-again affair with Chapur. After repeatedly asking him to end things with his Argentine paramour, she had finally had enough. In June 2009 she told Sanford that if he wouldn't end things, she wanted a divorce. Jenny Sanford, millionaire heiress to the "Stihl" power tool fortune, former Wall Street vice president, and all-around smart cookie, later said of her husband's decision to take a few days on the Appalachian Trail to hike and think: "I was hoping he was doing some real soul searching somewhere and devastated to find out it was Argentina. It's tragic." She has since filed for divorce.

Upon hearing of Sanford's tearful confession, one Republican South Carolina state senator said, "Lies, lies, lies. That's all we get from his staff. That's all we get from his people. That's all we get from him . . . . Why the big cover-up?"

Why, indeed.

Bastard.

JOHN EDWARDS
The End of the "Breck Girl"
(1953–)

> "[John] can try to treat the wound, and he has tried. He can try to make me less afraid, and he has tried. But I am now a different person."
> —Elizabeth Edwards

Before his election to one of North Carolina's U.S. Senate seats, John Edwards was known as the top trial lawyer in the state. He also was known as the "Breck Girl" for his fastidiousness about his hair and habit of spending $400 on haircuts. His first big win was in 1984 when a jury ordered a doctor to pay Edwards's client $3.7 million in damages in a case involving misuse of the anti-alcoholism drug Antabuse. From there, Edwards went on to secure the largest jury award in North Carolina history: $25 million for an improperly secured pool drain cover that resulted in a young child being disemboweled.

He soon leveraged his legal successes to gain political clout. In 1998, he ran as a Democratic challenger against ultraconservative Republican Senator Lauch Faircloth. Edwards was fighting an uphill battle. In the sixth year of President Bill Clinton's term, Democrats were expected to lose big, especially in the wake of the president's various sex scandals. This is not what happened. Democrats actually took back some of the ground they lost in 1994, and Edwards rode this wave into the Senate.

After his Senate term, Edwards was tapped by Massachusetts Senator John Kerry to be his running mate in the 2004 presidential election. The day after the election, Edwards announced that his wife had been diagnosed with breast cancer during the campaign.

He had been hailed by some as "the future of the Democratic party." He even ran a credible campaign for his party's presidential nomination, but could place no better than third in the crucial early primaries. During this time, his wife's cancer had spread to her lungs and bones.

And while his wife was battling terminal cancer, Edwards had an affair with one of his staffers, Rielle Hunter. It lasted for months. He and Hunter eventually had a daughter.

In late 2007, the *National Enquirer* began running reports that Edwards had cheated on his wife. While initially dismissing the reports, he admitted in late 2008 that he had indeed carried on an affair. Besides destroying him politically, Edwards's affair may land him in bigger trouble. He is currently being investigated by a federal grand jury on charges that he violated campaign finance laws by failing to disclose payments of hush money to Hunter.

BASTARD AND SAINT

So you're Elizabeth Edwards. You're a successful lawyer, smart as a whip, married to a flourishing, handsome politician, and you've been diagnosed with potentially terminal cancer. Talk about a mixed bag of outcomes. To top off the cocktail, your famous spouse knocks up a campaign worker, supposedly having agreed to marry her once you've died! What woman doesn't throw a louse like that one out?

> *"As we speak, [John]'s in El Salvador helping to build homes with the Fuller Center and Homes from the Heart. He cares about these issues, things that I care about. He's been a marvelous father. He really cared for me when I was sick, and really for the last thirty years. He made this one mistake. So do I throw out all the good stuff and say, 'That doesn't matter; only this matters'?"*
>
> —Elizabeth Edwards

INDEX

on earned his BA in History from Gonzaga University and both his BAE
d MA (History) from Eastern Washington University. Since entering the teach-
ion in 1993, he has taught at every level from sixth grade through college, serving
ety of committees, and mentoring countless junior and student teachers. He is the author of
g teams, and *Everything® Kids' States Book*, *The Everything® Kids' Presidents Book*, *Teacher Miracles*, and
uthor of *101 Things You Didn't Know about Lincoln*. He lives in Kent, WA.

W
Wri
Wyne